TECH TO SAVE
THE WORLD

TECH TO SAVE *the* World

A GUIDE TO HOW YOU CAN CHANGE THE WORLD

ASHLEY NICHOLS

NEW DEGREE PRESS

COPYRIGHT © 2021 ASHLEY NICHOLS

All rights reserved.

TECH TO SAVE THE WORLD

A Guide to How You Can Change the World

ISBN   978-1-63676-462-7   *Paperback*
          978-1-63676-463-4   *Kindle Ebook*
          978-1-63676-464-1   *Ebook*

CONTENTS

1

TECH WON'T SAVE THE WORLD—YOU WILL

THE DARKEST NIGHT

A young mother-to-be walked home from her village market as the sun lazily drifted away beyond the horizon. As she reached for her door, the last rays of light grazed her shoulders and disappeared into the coming night. She stepped inside, set down her bags, and paused. She felt a lurch and wrapped her arms around her stomach with a cry.

It was time.

Her family rushed her to the village medical clinic, but the dark of the night worked against her. The clinic had no power and no light. The doctor tried to work quickly, lighting candles and gathering what few supplies she could: cold water, cloth, a cell phone with only minutes of battery remaining. As the night grew darker, it was clear something was wrong.

She cursed to herself as she drew a candle closer to try to find the source of the problem, but its weak light wasn't strong enough. The doctor readied herself, fearing the night would unfold like many others before it. As the hours toiled on, so too did mother and child's efforts, both to little avail.

Finally, after a long, futile fight, they slipped into the darkness of the night together.

In the swollen silence that followed, the doctor placed a sheet over the mother's body. One by one, she blew out the candles. Looking out the window into the pitch beyond, she saw her reflection in the last of the flickering light. If only she had had some light; if only the child had come during the day.

A LABOR OF LOVE

Every year, more than three hundred thousand women die from pregnancy and childbirth complications. Many of these deaths occur in Africa and Asia. Obstetrician Dr. Laura Stachel was conducting research in Nigeria to understand why when the shadows of dark nights like this one whispered to her, drawing her down an uncharted path that would come to change her life and the world.

One evening, when she was working in a local medical clinic, the power went out before sunset. The local doctors explained power outages and rolling blackouts were very common in the region. Patients who came in at night were often turned away and told to find another medical provider; in some cases, those needing care would visit up to five clinics or hospitals in hopes of finding treatment.

Very ill patients had to wait for the sun to rise to receive lifesaving care. As night fell, health care providers would cobble together flashlights and phone screens trying to provide emergency care or support nighttime births. If a woman began to give birth during the night, she and her child were three times more likely to die together in the dark.

"Tears welled in my eyes," wrote Dr. Stachel in her thesis *Where There Is No Light.* "At that moment, I thought about all the women like her, suffering in silence and fighting for survival in health centers lacking even the most basic requirement for healthcare: light."

Frustrated and hoping to help in some way, Dr. Stachel sent a long email to her husband, Hal Aronson, the next day. Hal had been working in the solar energy space for ten years; she wondered if they could somehow work together to make a difference. Hal wrote back to her almost immediately, brainstorming ways to bring reliable power to the hospital.

Leveraging their joint expertise in the fields of medicine and solar power, they created a small, off-grid solar electric system that could be hand-carried to the hospital where Dr. Stachel was conducting research. They named the prototype the Solar Suitcase. The standalone electric system used solar energy collection from the daytime sunlight to power critical built-in tools, including medical procedure lamps, headlights, infrared thermometers, fetal dopplers, rechargeable headlamps, cell phone chargers, and walkie talkies, all tools that could mean the difference between life and death during a birth procedure.

"With these systems, laboring women—and their care providers—would no longer have to be in darkness," said Dr. Stachel. And she was right. As of 2021, Solar Suitcases have been used in more than five thousand health centers around the world and have generated more than 175 million hours of medical light. Their efforts have aided in the births and care of nearly eight million newborns and mothers.

WHAT MAKES CHANGE?

When we hear a story like Dr. Stachel's, it can be easy to focus on the technology aspect. "There's a suitcase that uses solar panels to bring light to medical clinics around the world! It's helped millions of women and children, who might have otherwise died in the dark. Isn't that incredible?"

Stories like Laura's are why I first began writing *Tech to Save the World*. As a technology consultant, I was excited to write about how technology was going to save our world and tackle grand challenges like global poverty, health, and climate change. Like many people, I had an unspoken belief that technology was the answer to our problems and it was going to somehow save us.

As is the way of these things, I was absolutely wrong.

What I found through countless hours of research and interviews with inventors and innovators around the world is that technology alone can't do anything. It's just a tool. But it's a tool that can be used by people who have a vision for a better world and who are passionate about solving some of the greatest challenges that lie before us.

Technology as it exists today can only *enhance* the efforts we are already driven to make. It can't strategize, it can't dream, and it can't innovate. It can only set out to complete the tasks we set before it.

"We collaborate *with* our technologies," notes Michael Schrage, a researcher at the Massachusetts Institute of Technology. "Historically, how painters mixed paints, sculptors used chisels, and musicians worked with instruments to come up with different music creations has been a part of the human creative tradition since recorded time. One collaborates with one's instruments."

Technology isn't going to save us. **It's human creativity, ingenuity, hope, passion, and even idealism—paired with technology—that can save the world.**

WHO MAKES CHANGE?

When I began writing, I initially viewed the people behind these idealistic innovations as extraordinary. I saw them as being a different class of person, someone smarter with more expertise, experience, and resources than I could ever hope to achieve. *If it's not the technology that's the secret to success, it must be the people*, I thought.

Once again, I was wrong.

When I asked these innovators to share their stories with me, time and time again they focused on how they became interested in the problems they were solving. They shared how they learned along the way, where they struggled, where they found friends and competitors. While the stories I captured for this book are incredible, many of the people who shared them are everyday people who cared about a problem and just did their best to *try to help in some way.*

Collaborating with them helped me realize **anyone can find ways to use technology to build a better world.**

Think of it this way. In time travel stories, there's always a keen focus on whether or not the characters do something small to change the past that has exponential impacts on the future. If something so small can so consequentially change the future, why do so many of us feel powerless in the present?

We have the ability to change our future and to save—or destroy—our world.

You are a world changer. You just need a little bit of information and the courage to start.

YOU ARE A TECH PERSON

Listen, I understand, technology is intimidating. It's all around us, every moment of every day, and it's always in a state of change. We hear about new advancements on the news on an almost daily basis, featuring everything from rockets to robotics to solar power. Even people who are comfortable with technology have trouble keeping up with and understanding it all.

Time and time again, people have told me they couldn't possibly use technology to make a difference in the world because they're "just not a tech person." Even though many of us appreciate and enjoy tech like our smartphones, our apps, our GPS, our video games, and our email accounts, there's a sense of disconnect between using these tools and understanding them. We don't know quite how they work, but we know they work for us.

When we think of "tech people," we think of Elon Musk, Bill Gates, Jeff Bezos, and other titans of the tech world. We envision people who can build or code new technologies from the ground up, people with Computer Engineering degrees and offices full of screens and gadgets. Most of us view "tech people" as being technology experts.

But here's the thing. All of us are tech people.

You use technology every day. You use it to work, to talk to friends and family, to make friends, to talk about your interests, to watch your favorite shows, and to pay your bills. You may even be reading this book on your phone or computer.

You know how to use technology to complete tasks and to achieve goals. **That makes you a tech person.**

It's true there are some who are more technical in their thinking, in their career, or in their hobbies. Some people know what needs to be done to construct a robot, to code a new mobile app, to program artificial intelligence, or to design a wind turbine. But even while there are people who know and understand what needs to be done, very few can actually do everything that needs to be done to bring that vision to life on their own. A developer can't singlehandedly solve a grand challenge by working on it alone. People who create new technologies need to partner with others who have experience in the problem they're working to solve, who can test and try out the new idea, and who can train others on how it could be used.

YOUR UNIQUE STRENGTHS CAN MAKE A DIFFERENCE

Lack of confidence in technology skills is one of the reasons so many smart, capable, and passionate people believe themselves to "not be tech people." It's very human to be uncomfortable with what we don't understand and an even more human trait to dislike feeling lost or stupid. It's even common in some of our most prominent technology companies. In a 2018 study of more than ten thousand technology professionals, 58 percent of people (including employees of Apple, Facebook, and Uber) reported experiencing Imposter Syndrome.

I've been there. In the early years of my career, I found myself sitting in a crowded conference room, directly across from two software developers, my eyes as wide as saucers as they debated with one another about which coding language would be the best option for a system we were building.

Their conversation wound through a wide range of topics and terms I knew nothing about and didn't understand. I was supposed to be the "communications consultant" for the project, and as I tried to follow the conversation, I quickly found myself completely lost. Worse, I felt cold terror winding a knot in my chest. This was my *career*. How could I not understand what was going on? Was I stupid?

After more than twenty minutes of debate, I shook away the cobwebs and cleared my throat. "Sorry," I interrupted. "I know this is a silly question…"

It would turn out that simple phrase would lead to much of my personal and professional success in the years to follow.

"Does this really matter?" I asked. "I know there are differences in the tools you're recommending, but what really matters to the client is how it impacts their work. Which of those options will result in the best tool for them?"

As I asked the question, an uncomfortable silence settled around the small room. As the coders stared at me, I was once again reminded in technicolor that I was by far the most junior member of the team, and I had interrupted two of our company's leading technologists to ask what even *I* thought was a stupid question.

"You know, damn. When you put it like that, I'm not sure," one of the developers said, leaning back in his chair. "I hadn't really thought of it that way. Great point."

The technologists continued their conversation, but as they did so, they brought it down to Earth. When mentioning a technical concern, they would pause and explain it to me and the others in the room. In the minutes that followed, more of my colleagues chimed in, sharing insights about what our clients needed and the benefits they were hoping to get from the new technology tool. Within a few minutes, with those insights, the option that would be best for our clients became clear.

As I gathered my things to leave the meeting, my boss paused by my shoulder. "I know you said it was a silly question, but it had a big impact," he said.

Since that day, when interviewers have asked me what my greatest strength is, I've smiled as I shared it's "being willing to ask the stupid questions."

That courage—stupidity?—is one of my strengths, but you have your own.

It's a common tendency to overlook our own strengths or knowledge because there's always someone out there who is more of an expert or better at something than we are. But what I've found is no one has your exact same blend of experiences, interests, and talents. Your personal experiences are your own, and even in an environment where you are collaborating with likeminded people, that blend is likely unique! This gives you a unique perspective that could make all the difference in the world.

A LESSON FROM OUR PAST

If you ever need an example of how different background experiences can result in greater innovation and change, look no further than the Wright Brothers. Their record as the "fathers of flight" is highly contentious because many inventors had created flying machines before their world-renowned flight at Kitty Hawk. In fact, historical records more frequently refer to their well-known achievement as the "first powered, sustained, controlled heavier-than-air flight."

What actually made their invention a turning point for aviation wasn't the flight element, but their creation of a three-axis control mechanism that allowed the pilot to maneuver a flying craft. In fact, their initial US patent was not for a flying machine, but for the control mechanism that they referred to as a "new and useful improvement in Flying Machines."

Their idea for that mechanism, versions of which are still used in modern aircraft, was born of their experiences working in a bicycle shop they ran in Dayton, Ohio. The men who helped them build the first powered, heavier-than-air aircraft were the bicycle mechanics who worked alongside them. Their collaboration and determination changed the course of history and set us on a trajectory for the stars; only sixty-six years after their first flight, man would use the same principles of flight to step foot on the moon.

What I love most about the story of the Wright brothers is they didn't grow up as bicycle designers or repairmen. They actually began their careers as printers, writing a weekly newspaper and using a printing press to publish books. They only later went on to open a bicycle shop and learn about the mechanisms that would be instrumental in flying airplanes.

They weren't trained pilots who taught people to fly; they were a curious, resilient group of people who took on a seemingly impossible challenge.

In our modern day and age, it won't just be the tech titans who will find creative ways to help technology save the world. It will also be people like you.

GETTING STARTED

If you are passionate about solving one of our world's greatest challenges, then you can *absolutely* use technology to help you along the way. Tech is becoming more user-friendly and accessible by the day, giving more and more people the ability to use robust tools to test ideas and create solutions.

Tech to Save the World was written to be a conversational guide to changing the world. This book isn't just a collection of stories of other people out there making a difference; instead, it's a hands-on guide to show how **you** can use technology to **build a better world.**

This book is split out into three key sections.

IF WE LAY A STRONG ENOUGH FOUNDATION...

In realizing it will be people—not technology—who will save the world, I wanted to learn more about what makes changemakers successful. I interviewed more than twenty inventors, entrepreneurs, students, and academics to learn what made world-changing initiatives work. Time and time again, I found common threads that wove through each of the incredible innovation stories that wait for you in the chapters to follow.

These **Foundations of Idealistic Innovation** included:

- Purpose and Passion
- Framing the Problem
- Collaborating
- Listening to Stakeholders, Locals, and Users
- Iterating

In the Foundations chapters, we'll talk through examples of how these intangibles resulted in incredible outcomes and how you can use them in your innovations.

A LITTLE BIT OF THIS, A LITTLE BIT OF THAT

To help prepare you for your world-changing journey, **The Workshop** section features some key information you'll need to get started, including:

- Building Comfort with Technology: Building confidence in trying (and sometimes failing) to use tech to make a difference
- Design Thinking—Dreaming to Big Ideas: How you can use start-up brainstorming and problem-solving methods to dream up new ideas
- (Some Of) The Tools of Innovation: A brief explainer on popular technology tools in the 2020s

This section is designed to help you build your personal toolbox of inspiration and techniques to explore your own idealistic innovations. Sift through the content and pick and choose what's most interesting to you. Skip over anything that you already know or doesn't intrigue you.

STARTING TO BUILD

Finally, the last section of this book—the **Blueprints**—will offer step-by-step guides or recipes to starting your own projects to make the world a better place. Because every reader is going to come in with different backgrounds, experiences, and expertise, the content in these guides may not apply to everyone. That's why the final section is broken up by reader groups.

- Blueprint for Dreamers: A guide for readers with limited access to resources
- Blueprint for Professionals: A guide for readers who currently work in a setting with some financial or team support
- Blueprint for Executives: A guide for leaders who want to bring idealistic innovation into their business or non-profit work

YOU CAN CHANGE THE WORLD

"Once you know what you want, understand why you want it. Make sure you want it because there's something not that you should do, but something you must do," shared Stacy Abrams in a 2018 TED Talk.

"It has to be something that doesn't allow you to sleep at night unless you're dreaming about it; something that wakes you up in the morning and gets you excited about it; or something that makes you so angry, you know you have to do something about it. But know why you're doing it. And know why it must be done."

I believe all of us have a calling and a dream that keeps us up at night. And I know everyone works differently, has different talents and skills, and has a different passion. Some readers of this book will be inspired to go forth and gather a new team. Others will be inspired to tinker and share their idea online. Yet others will sign up to be a member of a hackathon team or register for a new class. However you begin to pursue your dream, my hope is that this book gives you the understanding of what makes the convergence of technology and dreaming so powerful.

Let's get to changing the world, together!

THE FOUNDATIONS OF IDEALISTIC INNOVATION

2

PUTTING PASSION TO WORK

———

THE TERROR OF THE CRUSH

Hidden camera footage showed the baby elephant, separated from her mother, who had been tied to tree trunks to keep her from escaping. The baby cried out—first in fear and confusion, then in pain and despair as the handlers began to beat her with clubs and spikes. She screamed in desperation, trying to get away, straining against the ropes.

The video continued. Timestamps showed the beatings continued for hours, then days. All of the fight fell out of the baby. She fell limp, but her body was held up by the ropes and the beating continued. She was offered no food, no water, no time to rest—just pain and the gift of fear.

Two days later, the elephant handlers stopped their assault. Slowly, carefully, they untied the baby. They offered her some water and food with kind words and gentle pats. They tied a rope around her neck and led her back to where her mother waited. The mother cried out to her baby, but the baby just gazed forward with no recognition in her eyes. Her fear of humans had replaced the deepest bond.

Satisfied, the handlers offered the baby another snack and then led her away. Beginning tomorrow, she would be trained to perform tricks in an elephant show and let humans ride on her back and neck.

She was broken. She had been crushed.

ONE WOMAN'S PASSION

Sangdeaun "Lek" Chailert was an animal rights activist whose love of Asian elephants stretched back to her childhood. She had grown up helping her grandfather, the village shaman, care for sick and wounded animals, including elephants that lived nearby.

Growing up in a hill tribe in Thailand, she knew how the elephants in circuses and at trekking camps—which were the country's tourism pride—had been trained to be so responsive to human commands. They had been taken away from their mothers as babies and subjected to the "panjan," or the crush. The horrible process immersed elephants into a world of terror and pain from which their minds would never truly recover. This break, and this life-long fear of humans, made the elephants more malleable and trainable.

In the early 2000s, Lek used hidden cameras to secretly film and photograph the panjan. After capturing the footage, she shared it with a *National Geographic* reporter who used the clips for a documentary series, and it spread like wildfire. Her impassioned pleas for people to stop frequenting circuses and other elephant tourism attractions echoed around the world, and doubt began to take root.

People began to question elephant care and training methods in Thailand and at animal shows in their own countries. This would later be a major factor in circuses worldwide shifting away from elephant and animal acts in their shows. People for the Ethical Treatment of Animals and other advocacy groups around the world called for tourists to boycott visiting Thailand until the panjan practice was stopped.

While attitudes began to shift around the globe, Lek's calls for change and advocacy made her an unpopular figure in Thailand. Her support of the tourism boycott drew the ire of government officials. She was publicly jailed multiple times. In what may have been the worst blow of all, her own family gave her an ultimatum. Either she would reach out to the media and take back what she had said, or they would disown her.

For Lek, there was never even a question of which path she would take. Her passion for saving elephants guided her through challenging times and she never recanted. She never backed down. She stood her ground and while she lost her human family, she found another in the animals she worked to rescue.

She would go on to found and establish Elephant Nature Park, one of Thailand's first elephant sanctuaries and rescue centers. Elephant Nature Park serves almost as a retirement home for elephants; many of the park's rescued elephants are sixty years old or older, and most have been purchased by Lek and brought to the park following long lives of working at logging camps or in animal tourism.

Elephant Nature Park is known around the world in part due to its volunteer support model. Leaning on social media, Lek invites people from around the world to visit the park and help care for the elephants she has rescued using the Internet and social media word of mouth. Each year, the park attracts thousands of volunteers, including solo travelers, school groups, and nature enthusiasts. All of these volunteers are told stories of the park's elephants by Lek or other members of her team and people are invited to share them through their own social media handles.

Today, Lek's passion for the care and conservation of Indian elephants is vibrant. Whether interacting with her online or in person, her conviction and love of the animals are contagious. She has continued to use technology through every step of her journey to funnel that passion into action. She has capitalized on social media to bring the plight of the elephants into the homes of people around the world and to help connect animal lovers millions of miles away with the creatures they love.

"The most powerful tool to saving the biggest giants on Earth can fit in the palm of your hand," Lek said, holding up her smartphone. Her passion for the gentle giants shines even in the crowded space of social media. In 2021, her assorted social media platforms have more than five hundred thousand followers worldwide.

In 2020, Thailand closed its borders to visitors in response to the COVID-19 pandemic. Suddenly, Elephant Nature Park lost a large swath of its day-to-day support as volunteers were unable to travel to the park. Even worse, elephant tourism attractions throughout the country completely and suddenly lost their revenue streams. There was no money to feed the thousands of captive elephants across the country.

Once again, Lek drew upon her passion and sense of purpose to endure the challenging times and help save suffering elephants. She launched Eleflix, a livestreamed video channel that used Facebook and Instagram to connect with people who were quarantining in their homes all over the world. She and her team of elephant keepers created new content almost daily, sharing information about elephant care, relationships, rescues, and more.

Her team established VIP Zoom calls where elephant lovers who were stuck at home during lockdowns could pay to receive a virtual tour of Elephant Nature Park and meet some of the residents. They also began selling elephant "birthday cakes," displays of nutrient-rich elephant food spelling out birthday wishes or congratulations to fans. The cakes were photographed, enjoyed by the elephants, and shared by Elephant Nature Park.

While never begging followers or fans for funding, in these broadcasts and posts, Lek continued to champion Indian elephants and was candid about the financial challenges the tourism lockdown brought to the park. She used a simple-to-use, cost-effective method to continue sharing her passion for the majestic creatures.

Social media followers and supporters donated throughout the pandemic, both through "elephant adoptions" that funded an elephant's food for a full year and through general donations. Collected funds went toward the upkeep and maintenance of Elephant Nature Park, upkeep of Lek's other elephant sanctuary projects, and to upskilling for her elephant keeper staff and their families who were financially struggling.

Lek and her team were not social media wizards. They didn't use search engine optimization or devote a huge budget to fancy marketing or pay for influencer promotions. Instead, they brought their true selves and their passion for their work to their online engagement across Facebook, YouTube, and Instagram. They poured their love for elephants and animals into their posts and livestreams, and that helped support the organization and its animals at a time when many other nonprofits floundered.

Steve Jobs once said, "You have to be burning with an idea, or a problem, or a wrong that you want to right. If you're not passionate enough from the start, you'll never stick it out." Lek's work in elephant conservation and education is an incredible story of a passionate woman using everyday technologies to right what once appeared to be an insurmountable wrong.

YOUR PASSION, YOUR PURPOSE

Like Lek, all of us have that little flame that burns bright in our hearts. It is a flicker of compassion, of a desire for things to be different, of a wish for change that we know just can't be granted.

That small fire is passion. All of us have something that we are passionate about, that we deeply believe in. Perhaps you're passionate about climate change or ending homelessness. Maybe some part of you wants to save the sharks (increasingly endangered due to the popularity shark fin soup) or help children learn to read. Whatever topic makes your flame flicker with energy and excitement, you have some passion within you.

Passion is a bit of a fickle thing. It can come and go. It can grow into a roaring fire after reading a story, or dim after a few months of us focusing on life's many demands. But I believe passion doesn't ever go away; it just goes dormant, waiting for us to take notice of it again, and to put it to good use.

Usually we're at least somewhat knowledgeable about the things we care about, even if that's a result of curiosity, interest bias, or our prior experiences. It can be easy to brush aside our own understanding (and even expertise) in these topics because there's always someone else out there who is more educated or more experienced in them. But what I've learned throughout my career in education, government, consulting, and technology is that people who are passionate about certain problems are often the first to identify new opportunities to solve them.

Being willing to apply our passions to grand challenges and think creatively about how we can solve them with existing and up-and-coming technologies is going to be the key to building a better world. That passion can fuel belief in ourselves, and in each other, to create new ideas that can change the world.

While it may seem warm and fuzzy, passion plays a concrete role in idealistic innovation. In a paper released in the *Academy of Management Review,* researchers discovered "[p]assion involves strength and courage, mobilizing energy, and unflagging pursuit of challenging goals. [It] has been related to drive, tenacity, willingness to work long hours, courage, high levels of initiative, and persistence in the face of obstacles."

In another 2018 study on the concept of grit, researchers also found that passion plays a key role in helping us stay focused on our goals, persevering through challenging days, and results in better overall performance.

If you're reading this book, my suspicion is this chapter is the reason you picked it up in the first place. You're here, still reading, because you want to make a difference in the world. Like Lek, and like many others, you want to work hard at work worth doing.

What you may not realize is this passion, and this commitment, has the potential to be one of your greatest strengths as you dive into the world of technology and innovation.

PURPOSE BURNS BRIGHT AND DRAWS OUT LIGHT IN OTHERS

For Fabien Cousteau, conserving and learning from our oceans isn't just his passion, it's his birthright. His grandfather,

Jacques Cousteau, was a world-famous marine researcher and aquanaut. His family has been inspiring people around the world to love and care for our oceans for more than fifty years.

Even though the Cousteaus have changed the way we look at our oceans, we've still explored less than 5 percent of them. Hoping to change that, Fabien began to explore ways to create underwater research centers that would help divers with exploration and research. When the sea itself offered no answers, he looked to the skies.

Inspired by the International Space Station, Fabien announced his vision for PROTEUS in 2020. PROTEUS will be "an underwater space station that is bigger than any underwater research location in history." The size of a large house, it is planned to include research spaces, scientific laboratories, sleeping quarters, and the first underwater greenhouse. It will also feature continuous live video streaming for education and augmented and virtual reality experiences for students and other surface dwellers. The station will be powered sustainably with wind, solar, and thermal energy.

The research station will allow scientists and aquanauts to dive far more frequently and for longer time spans than they would normally be able to, particularly at night. The habitat will allow for potential discoveries of new species of marine life, enable better understanding of climate change's effect upon the ocean, and will create opportunities to test new technologies related to green power, aquaculture, engineering, and robotic exploration.

When I met with Fabien, I was ready to dive into details about the specific technologies that would be used to make his vision a reality. I had more questions than time and I couldn't wait to get more details. Imagine my surprise when I joined the meeting and found Fabien was almost as excited to meet with me as I was with him. His excitement about the project was contagious, and not just to me.

"We did closed sessions with experts to feel out the project idea and get feedback," shared Cousteau. "The first time we did one of these conventions, I was fully expecting a lot of people—a lot of these amazing people from the Navy, higher education institutions, and experts in exploration—to say 'this is crazy, it's impossible, or impractical' or what have you. Universally, not a single person was resistant to the idea. If anything, they were extraordinarily excited by this."

The reasoning behind this shared excitement varied. "PROTEUS is a hopeful step forward in spreading the message that we must protect the ocean as if our lives depend on it," said Dr. Sylvia Earle, American marine biologist and *National Geographic* explorer-in-residence. "Living underwater gives us the gift of time and the incredible perspective of being a resident on the reef. You're not just a visitor anymore."

"PROTEUS will transform how we conduct underwater science and engineering," said Dr. Mark Patterson, Associate Dean for Research and Graduate Affairs in the College of Science at Northeastern University.

But beneath all the dazzling shine of the possibilities and potential, the heart of the PROTEUS project is Fabien's passion for a purpose his family has been supporting for generations.

"The world needs healing," he shared. "We don't need any more division. As my grandfather used to say, 'If we're going to get out of this, we all need to roll in the proverbial same direction, we're all in the same boat.' Nature doesn't care what we think or what side of the political spectrum we're on. We depend on nature; nature does not depend on us. For us to be able to cater to our life support system, we all have to unify and bear together and [PROTEUS] will hopefully be one of those platforms that helps that process."

STARTING WITH "WHY" IS ESSENTIAL TO SUCCESS

Cousteau's PROTEUS project is a quintessential example of how staying focused on your passion or purpose and "starting with why," a term coined by author and speaker Simon Sinek, is powerful to a project's success.

"Very few people or companies can clearly articulate *why* they do *what* they do," writes Sinek. "When I say *why*, I don't mean to make money—that's a result. By *why*, I mean what is your purpose, cause, or belief? *Why* does your company exist? *Why* do you get out of bed every morning? And *why* should anyone care?"

Focusing on your purpose or "the why" can help ensure your passion continues to shine through, even in the face of barriers, obstacles, or bureaucracy. It can help you to connect with others of different backgrounds and skill sets who are passionate about a similar issue or cause. Cursory knowledge about the challenge you're hoping to solve will help you better connect with—and recruit—others with similar passions to your team, and they'll be in the trenches with you to solve the problem.

It can also help you communicate about the work you're doing to solve the problem. As you're working to recruit team members, gather funding, or get the attention of stakeholders whose support you'll need, understanding and leveraging your own passion and purpose will be key.

"We've built an underwater research center that will let us do lots of scientific research" is less moving than "we've built an underwater space station that will help us better understand and protect our oceans, which matters because our life depends on them." While both are true of Cousteau's PROTEUS project, one rings a bit truer because it doesn't focus on the what. It starts with the why.

PUTTING PASSION INTO PRACTICE

Karine Toumazeau, founder of Blue Stark Strategy, is a young professional who took her love for conservation and turned it into action. She now works as consultant for nonprofit organizations, helping them apply lessons learned from her background in the business world to broaden their impact.

"Right now, you have a new generation of leaders who are selfless and who are ready to work for the common good," Karine shared. "I'm confident that my generation will have the moral compass to do the right thing and reinvent the rules."

Karine isn't the only one shifting her professional focus to making the world a better place. One of her clients, a nonprofit called Coral Gardeners, has found success in recruiting brilliantly talented technologists from around the world by giving them the opportunity to make a difference in conservation. "We attract people from the private sector, even from the Silicon Valley. Engineers who worked at Tesla or Uber come and we start to have these amazing conversations about building technology for the ocean. They come to us and say, 'I can do my job for a good cause.'"

Of course, not all of us can fulfill our passions through our day jobs. That doesn't mean we can't do something to find fulfillment in our spare time, such as working on a passion project or teaming up with friends to try and solve a challenging problem.

I'll use myself as an example. My passion was nudged in fall 2020 at the height of the worldwide COVID pandemic. I felt listless, lost, and powerless. I wanted so badly to help and be able to do something, somewhere, some*how*. Everything felt like it was falling apart and there was nothing I could do. Then, I came across an article about how a team at the technology company Accenture was using artificial intelligence to save coral reefs.

That sparked my interest and gave me something to smile about. I wanted to learn more. I started to research the program, and then I started to research others. I began reaching out for interviews. I began talking to people around me about these incredible uses of technology, and when people told me they wish they knew how they could "do something like that," I started to share notes and ideas with them.

Those thoughts and ideas turned into *Tech to Save the World*. It turns out my passion is helping other people find the tools they need to leap into the unknown and try using technology about what *they* are passionate about. Of course, I was continuing to work my day job as a technology consultant, but I fed my passion on nights and weekends in the hopes it might make a difference for someone.

When was the last time you thought, *Somebody should do something about that?*

Maybe that "somebody" should be you.

Harriet Tubman once said, "Every great dream begins with a dreamer. Always remember, you have within you the strength, the patience, and the passion to reach for the stars to change the world."

We talked earlier about how each of us has different experiences and passions. Your passion, the thing (or things) that excites or frustrates you or keeps you up at night, is all yours. It is unique to you. It is a gift, a boon you can use to propel you from wishing things were different to making them different yourself.

Put it to good use.

3

FRAMING THE PROBLEM

THE ~~GOLDEN~~ GOSSAMER GOOSE

In 1959, British mogul Henry Kremer posed a question. In a time when planes were powered by gas and electricity to fly, could an aircraft powered by human energy alone fly a substantial distance? He offered a prize of fifty thousand pounds to the first team that could fly their human-powered aircraft through a one-mile-long course and one hundred thousand pounds to the first to fly across the English Channel. Teams around the world, from aerospace companies to university research and development groups, began building.

The prizes went unclaimed for *eighteen years.*

As the years passed, one by one, the teams working to build airplanes that could meet the challenge gave up on the effort. Human-powered flight was an interesting idea, but it just didn't seem feasible. The teams would spend months—sometimes up to a year—theorizing, designing the aircraft, and building them. Then, when the planes were rolled out for their first flights, they would almost immediately crash. Teams would return to the drawing board, spending months repairing the craft and trying to find new ways to solve the problem.

The dream of human-powered flight seemed dead.

Meanwhile, in the United States, an aeronautical engineer named Paul MacCready was in a bit of a pickle. He had cosigned a business loan for a friend. When the business went belly up, he found himself in thousands of dollars of debt.

You might say he was passionate about getting out of debt.

With that motivation driving him onward, MacCready turned his gaze to the impossible challenge of the fifty-thousand-pound Kremer Prize. He began by looking at what his predecessors had tried and where they had failed.

He was hit by a sudden realization. "The problem is we don't *understand* the problem," he said.

Human-powered flight was an effort that was going to require iteration; repeated tests of the aircraft were needed to gather information and tweak the prototypes. Teams were spending years between each test flight to perfect their ideas instead of testing them.

Everyone was trying to solve the problem of human-powered flight. But to solve *that* problem, MacCready focused on creating an aircraft that could be rebuilt within a matter of hours. When he rolled out his first prototype for a test it crashed immediately, but he was able to check what had gone wrong and iterate.

This cycle repeated again and again and again. MacCready became so efficient at repairing and testing his planes that he was able to fly up to four test flights a day. It took him only six months to claim the fifty-thousand-pound Kremer prize for his Gossamer Condor aircraft and the one-hundred-thousand-pound prize for his Gossamer Albatross a year later.

SOLVING FOR THE RIGHT PROBLEMS

Paul MacCready's human-powered aircrafts were successful because he didn't focus his energies on the problem everyone else was trying to solve. Instead, he stepped back to look at the challenge from a different angle and avoided one of the common pitfalls in idealistic innovation. Often, as a team works together to find an answer to a problem, they can become so wrapped up in the intricacies of the proposed solution that they lose sight of the problem being solved for.

"It's understandable that we leap to solutions," writes Daniel Markovitz, author of *The Conclusion Trap*. "[F]ixing problems provides a dopamine surge that is comforting, especially when the world around us feels more volatile and threatening. Nevertheless, an ineffective Band-Aid solution can make things worse, and can be just as damaging in the long run as the problem it's trying to solve."

We see this time and again when trying to make the world a better place. Complex issues like education, homelessness, conservation, and climate change can't be solved by a silver bullet, and many times people disagree on how they can and *should* be solved.

These problems can be daunting, and not just because they're hard to fix. After all, if experts and nonprofits committed to them haven't been able to solve them, what could we possibly do? But we may bring a new perspective, which gives us an opportunity to do something new that could make all the difference.

Before we begin problem-solving, we have to understand the source of the problem. This is often more challenging said than done. Humans are problem-solvers, but we tend to like simple answers that we can use to our advantage. "The truth is that you will seek what you set yourself up to seek and you will find what you set yourself up to find," writes Paloma Cantero-Gomez for *Forbes*. "Making an effort to examine the potential challenge as to understand it fully in its essence and implications is time well-spent."

UNDERSTANDING THE PROBLEM

Albert Einstein famously said, "If I had an hour to solve a problem, I'd spend fifty-five minutes thinking about the problem and five minutes thinking about solutions." The longer we think about and explore a problem, the better we understand it, and the better equipped we are to do something about it.

But what do we do with that time? Circling around our current understanding for an hour won't get us anywhere and won't help us understand the problem at a deeper level.

Deconstructing a challenge and identifying its nuances and root causes can be done in many ways. A few of the exercises in Chapter 9 "Design Thinking—Dreaming to Big Ideas" can help you and your team dig deeper, check your assumptions, and test your gut instinct solution ideas. Try different ways of describing or explaining the problem. "If you see that your problem statement has only one solution, rethink it," continues Markovitz. "Begin with observable facts, not opinions, judgments, or interpretations."

Next, ask for help! Reach out to experts and academics to request their expertise, learn more about the topic, and pulse your level of understanding of the issue. Ask them to share feedback on your team's thinking so far—positive *or* constructive. Similarly, make some time to connect with the people who are directly impacted.

You can also test your own understanding of the problem by trying the 40-20-10-5 exercise. To test yourself and your team, start by stating the problem in forty words or less. Then, state the problem again in only twenty words. State it again in ten words and one last time in five words. Although we are solving for complex problems, this exercise can challenge you to understand the heart of the issue.

As you continue to learn more, begin considering possible solutions, and be excited about "being wrong." It can be difficult to let go of an idea or prototype that we've worked so hard to craft, but sometimes our early ideas don't address the true problem. Being willing to set ideas aside will prevent your team from churning on a solution that is never going to be effective.

"There's [an] advantage to redefining your problem: it frees you to experiment with 'beginner's mind,'" writes Peter Bregman, CEO of Bregman Partners and best-selling author of *18 Minutes*. "You get to start over, trying different solutions, assessing their effectiveness, learning from failures, and trying again."

TECHNOLOGY MAY NOT BE THE *RIGHT* TOOL

When we're looking to solve problems, if we frame the problem in such a way that technology is the obvious answer, the effort is more likely to fail. With the rise of technology has come a new challenge: the perception of tech as a silver bullet. That's not to say that technology isn't a powerful tool. It can be, but only if used correctly and to solve for specific problems rather than symptoms of those problems.

That's another reason why it's important to put the **problem first** when looking for solutions.

Notice I didn't use the phrase "technology solutions." When we can, we should solve problems in a technology agnostic way and pull in technology when it offers value and an opportunity to amplify our human impact.

As a consultant, I have seen it firsthand many times. In our technology-filled world, it's all too easy to try to make a tech tool solve for a problem when it just doesn't fit. When those situations arise, we have a few options. We can either continue to try and force a square peg into a round hole, or we can recognize we've made a mistake.

When we choose the latter, we can pause and take a step back. We can revisit the problem we're trying to solve for. We can reframe the question. Once we understand the root of the problem, our chances of solving for it increase exponentially.

As Astro Teller, Captain of Moonshots at X the Moonshot Factory (formerly Google X), notes, "Fall in love with the problem, not the solution." X is a company designed to invent and launch "moonshot" technologies that aim to make the world a radically better place, and its employees have a wide range of backgrounds, skill sets, and passions.

"[T]echnology is the tool, not the end game," shares a company representative. "If we catch ourselves spending a lot of time refining a new technology and saying, 'This could be great for lots of things…someday' without an idea of how to make it so, that's usually a bad sign. Instead, we want to fall in love with a problem and aim to understand it so deeply that it becomes easier to find fresh new approaches."

THE WISDOM OF THE CROWD

No one loves a good problem as much as Alex Kim, founder of Crowdsolv. A technology consultant and policy wonk, Alex struggled to balance his passion for making the world a better place and the increasingly complex nature of some of our global challenges. "I started going down that path of cynicism, [that] all these problems were too complicated," shared Alex. "I don't think there's anybody in the world—no expert, no one—who knows the full solutions to these challenges we have."

He was frustrated and disappointed by the social discord that flowed around issues like homelessness, police brutality, gun control, and the pandemic response. His attempts to discuss or learn more about the nuances on the topics using social media like Facebook or Twitter were met with toxicity and vitriol for other perspectives. Alex asked himself, "How can we communicate better to solve challenges?"

As he looked to solve the problem, his initial conversations with friends and colleagues were fruitless; most people agreed it was human nature to disagree so fiercely and dislike others with differing opinions. But then something shifted.

"When I looked at things like Wikipedia and open-source software, I saw all of these ways that we collaborate, for free, and how as humans we can do a really amazing job of working together. If I go pull the Wikipedia article for something, chances are it's going to be balanced, fleshed out, and not too extreme. We always say it's impossible for us to work together on political and social challenges, but we work so well together in an open fashion in so many other ways. What's the difference?"

Through further research, Alex determined that many of the tools we use to discuss these challenges, particularly social media, weren't built to enable productive discussion. His new problem became "what kind of space do we need for thousands of people to collaborate effectively?"

In response, he quit his lucrative job as a data scientist to build a new platform designed to help people around the world collaborate to dive into the root causes of problems and crowdsource solutions. The platform enabled communication and established a framework for breaking down issues into distinct root causes. Crowdsolv.org launched in early 2021, issuing a challenge to keyboard warriors everywhere.

"Across comments sections, forums, question-and-answer sites, and academic journals, everyone thinks they know the 'secret' to solving some of life's toughest challenges," reads the Crowdsolv website. "Unfortunately, these challenges still haven't been solved." While the site is still in its infancy as of this book's publication, contributors from around the Internet have begun to share their unique ideas, perspectives, and framing for complex problems.

As solutions continue to be developed, Alex's long-term goal is to use those insights and ideas to draft legislation for state and local governments. "We can take the solutions that people make on the site and we can translate them into bills that can be implemented. That closes the loop between something that's an academic exercise and something that could actually become real."

SAVING THE REEFS WITH PHOTOS OF FISH?

Similarly, reframing the problem was one of the keys to success for Philippe Daniel's work on Project CORaiL, an artificial intelligence tool that can be used to monitor coral reef health. A project lead at worldwide technology company Accenture, Philippe was a leader of the company's diving club. During a trip to a diving convention, he met representatives from a nonprofit who restored coral reefs that had been damaged by dynamite fishing in the Philippines.

Many village fishermen around the world use dynamite or other explosives to stun or kill fish and collect them when they float to the top. This has been particularly harmful in the Philippines; according to the *Philippine Journal of Science*, none of the country's reefs are in "excellent" condition. Worse, more than 90 percent are in poor or fair condition.

Learning about the coral preservation efforts inspired Philippe and a colleague to begin volunteering with the nonprofit organization. They began by helping regrow coral and monitoring the remaining reefs. At the time, the nonprofit was focused on the problem of blast fishing. How could they stop or reduce the practice in the region? Local fishermen preferred it to traditional fishing methods, even though it was illegal.

While helping to repair some of the broken reefs, Philippe and his team began to think about the problem differently. They found themselves asking, "How can we help regrow the coral that's been damaged? How would we know those efforts were successful?"

In discussions with the nonprofit, they learned one of the keys to coral reef repair is observation. Conservationists dive down to reefs to identify the most resilient coral to use for regrowth. While on the dives, they would also photograph the local sea life. "They would try to count the number of fish, identify the different species, and see if they were mature," shared Philippe. The health of local fish populations is a strong indicator of reef health.

Of course, observation by diving came with its own challenges. Checking reefs can be dangerous, time intensive, and disruptive to the very reef ecosystems that researchers are working to preserve. Most fish and sea life would scatter when a diver approached, making it challenging to get a good picture of the underwater community. Philippe and his team wondered if they could use technology and their backgrounds in artificial intelligence to help solve the new problem of how to count fish.

"We decided to see if we could help them to monitor the reef using automated cameras to help them monitor the growth of the fish population." This instantaneous, unmanned photography could help the nonprofit monitor fish populations, observe their behaviors without interruption, and even monitor sediments in the water.

Project CORaiL uses underwater cameras that are set up to detect movement and automatically take a photo when a fish swims by. The photos are then reviewed by an artificial intelligence algorithm, which counts and classifies the types of marine life present at the reef. After crunching the numbers, the artificial intelligence algorithm shares its findings with a dashboard that automatically updates for the nonprofit, allowing researchers to frequently check the health of the reef.

By focusing on the problem of how to count fish to monitor reef health, and tweaking their solution to address the challenge, Philippe and his teammates were able to create an artificial intelligence tool that would learn more about the reef the longer it was used. In its first year, the intelligent camera automatically captured and categorized seventy thousand images of fish. It would have taken divers months of dive time to gather the same number of photos and insights.

DIG A LITTLE DEEPER

Our world is becoming increasingly complex, and our challenges only more so. To turn our passion into action and truly make a difference, the best way to begin is by learning more and questioning everything we think we know.

We're guaranteed to learn more along the way. And, just maybe, along the way we'll find our own ~~golden~~ gossamer goose.

4

COLLABORATING

THREADS OF FATE

In La Paz, Bolivia, children were dying.

Heart conditions are more common at high altitudes due to lower levels of oxygen. In La Paz, which rests twelve thousand feet above sea level, children are ten times more likely to be born with congenital heart defects than others born elsewhere in the world. In 2010, the UN found that Bolivia suffered from the highest infant mortality rate in South America.

When Dr. Franz Freudenthal began practicing medicine in La Paz, there were few treatment options for the sick children who were brought to him. The most common heart defect, an opening between two major blood valves, could only be addressed through expensive medical devices or through open heart surgery. The residents of La Paz had limited access to medical care and couldn't afford the lifesaving surgeries, leaving them with no way to help their dying children.

After seeing the death of a newborn, Dr. Freudenthal began to look for creative ways to treat the heart defects. He turned his gaze to medical devices, and over time invented the non-invasive Nit Occlud device.

A single piece of woven noncorroding wire, Nit Occlud can be used to close the holes in a child's heart using a catheter and without open heart surgery. The wire is made of nitinol, an intricate material that can memorize a shape and retain it even after being folded and inserted.

Although Dr. Freudenthal's early tests of the device were successful, there was one major challenge. Because it was intricately woven using one long piece of fine wire, there was no way to mass-produce the devices in Bolivia. They had to be handwoven. He reached out to the only people who could help—the very women whose children were dying.

Approximately 70 percent of Bolivians are descendants of an Indigenous group known as the Aymara, and many of the artistic and weaving traditions passed down by those ancestors are still used today. The weaving traditions were more commonly used for knitting clothes and blankets. "The women who work here are Aymara and carry the ability to weave in their blood," said Dr. Freudenthal.

After learning how to craft the different versions of the device, the women quickly got to work, weaving the difference between life and death for the children of La Paz. "The engineers bring their knowledge and systemization and the artists bring their ability and their art, and that's how they produce these devices," said Dr. Freudenthal.

They're making all the difference. Since 2007, the rate of premature death due to heart defects has dropped 36 percent in Bolivia. The device has been found to be a safe and effective treatment for closing holes in the heart, with a 97 percent success rate in children.

"It seems beautiful to me that this ancestral weaving, together with this technology, is saving kids," shared Dr. Freudenthal.

"For me, it's a miracle."

WE CAN'T DO IT ALONE

When we think of innovation, we often think of the people who are considered technology titans of our time. Jeff Bezos, Elon Musk, Bill Gates, and Steve Jobs are all touted as one-man bands, or what Shira Ovide terms singular geniuses. "It's the audacious, maybe slightly off-kilter, sharp-elbowed technology genius who makes all the magic happen," she writes for the *New York Times.*

I think we can agree that when these tech titans set the pace for technological advancements and innovation, it can feel like everyday people like us have little to offer the world by comparison.

What I find interesting is that none of them built their technology and innovation empires alone.

That's right. Not a single one.

Instead, they collaborated with other people or larger teams to bring their visions to life. Yes, sometimes they were the visionary behind the efforts, but none of them went it alone. "It was Wozniak and Jobs. It was Hewlett and Packard. Jeff Bezos would literally be the first to talk about how he created a strong team," shares MIT Fellow and innovation author Michael Schrage. "If it's not a collaborative relationship, it's an individual who seeks to create a collaborative community. The whole notion of collaborative ethos is core to scalable, iterative innovation."

Just like Dr. Freudenthal and the Aymara weavers, the tech titans benefit from collaboration with teammates and partners who bring unique backgrounds and expertise to the table. While there's something romantic about going it alone, finding the right team to work *with* toward a common goal is key to tackling big challenges and saving the world.

Research into project and workplace collaboration gives us some insight into why it is so impactful. According to *Forbes Magazine,* "Participants [who acted] collaboratively stuck at their task 64 percent longer than their solitary peers, whilst also reporting higher engagement levels, lower fatigue levels, and a higher success rate." Other studies have shown "[w]orkplace collaboration can increase successful innovation by 15 percent."

Meanwhile, lack of collaboration can result in less than desired results. A survey by Salesforce found "86 percent of employees and executives cite lack of collaboration or ineffective communication for workplace failures."

From the numbers, it's clear that collaboration is key to idealistic innovation, but why?

BANDING TOGETHER TO DEFEAT DEATH ITSELF

One incredible example of the surprisingly collaborative "solo genius" is Tyler Hayes, CEO of Atom Limbs. He founded the company to create bionic prostheses that provide a wider range of use than traditional prosthetics, beginning with arms. His long-term dream is to help humans conquer death. He knew if his new company was to truly advance humanity, the old ways of working wouldn't work anymore.

"When I was young, I taught myself to code and build websites. I sold design and coding services and built websites for people, and I thought it was the best thing ever. I would think, 'I can work independently, and no one could tell me what to do.' And honestly, it was nice, especially as a teenager. It was a huge level of autonomy that most people don't get even as an adult. But one thing that came from that was *industrial level arrogance.*"

Tyler was good at what he did because he knew it well and could creatively think through challenges that came his way. From the time he started his first company coding websites to his early work as a founder in the start-up world, he had a habit of working independently without collaborating with others on his team, or his clients. "I would throw work over the wall; it was a terrible way to build anything!"

As his working world expanded from websites to starts-ups and, later, prosthetic devices, it became clear that he could no longer go it alone. A few months after founding Atom Limbs, he implemented what he and his team refer to as the 20/80 framework.

"If you're working on a project, when you get 20 percent in, you announce the work that you've done so far. You come to everyone at the company, and everyone gives you notes," said Tyler. Members of the company would share their initial ideas and work and take constructive feedback from their peers who have different backgrounds and skill sets before continuing their efforts.

"It's then your job to take that feedback and amp this thing up or turn this thing down. We check in again at 80 percent. Ultimately, what always happens at 80 percent is that we feel way better than we did at 20 percent because we made some deviation that we're glad we made."

The feedback and insight from their colleagues with different backgrounds and areas of expertise allows the researchers at Atom Limbs to build more reliable, more effective prosthetic limbs and brings Tyler's team closer to their vision of curing death.

MAKING COLLABORATION WORK

Even though we know collaboration is important, it doesn't make it easy. When we're passionate about a project or idea, it can be challenging to share that vision with a broader team who may want to change it in some way. When a group works together, different working styles and opinions can cause conflict that can distract from the team's mission. Group work is often slower than individual work, and one person's slower pace can slow down everyone's efforts. It can be a struggle to even find people to collaborate with in the first place.

How can we make sure that our team works well, together, to make a difference in the world?

DREAM BIGGER TO INSPIRE ACTION

Defeating death and saving children are grand challenges that inspire people. These challenges reach into their hearts and urge them to bring their very best. "The surest way to get remarkably talented (even egocentric) people to collaborate is to give them a problem, a challenge that is worth collaborating around," says Michael Schrage. In an interview about collaboration, he encouraged everyday people to pursue challenges that inspire the teams around them.

Many collaborations are minor, focused on reducing costs by a few percentage points or increasing market share. Very few people truly want to bring their best to solve such incremental problems. "Pick a challenge. Pick an opportunity. Pick a problem that invites and excites collaboration that people unhesitatingly say, 'Yes, that's the kind of thing I'm prepared to sacrifice a bit of my ego to work with other talented people to solve,'" Michael urges. "Who did a great job of that? Steve Jobs. Mark Zuckerberg."

DIFFERENT STRENGTHS MAKE US STRONGER

In addition to a culture of collaboration and a problem worthy of solving, another element of successful collaboration is mutual recognition of talents, skill sets, and strengths. It turns out that having diverse teams in terms of gender, ethnic background, and experiences helps teams perform better.

McKinsey & Company, a management consulting firm, studied the impact of diversity on team performance in 2015. They found that companies that had higher than average gender and ethnic diversity were likely to financially outperform their industry peers and competitors.

In the business world, there are countless "workstyle personality" tests and quizzes to help managers pull together high performing teams. Gallup StrengthsFinder, Meyers Briggs, and Social Styles are a few of the common tools used by companies to try to find the right mix for teams. Why would that be, if there wasn't strength in a team effort rather than a solo one?

There's power in diversity of working styles and strengths, and there's also power in each individual team member understanding what they bring to the table.

That understanding is a key element. When I was a graduate student studying Higher Education, one of my professors wanted our cohort to have a better understanding of ourselves, our working styles, and how we worked with teams as we prepared to enter the workforce. She had us take a "working personality profile" test and brought in an expert on the different personas to talk to us about our findings. The test has changed in the years that have passed, but at the time it used three colors to define working personalities:

- Red workstyles were people who often took charge, led projects, and managed others
- Blue workstyles were people who focused on emotional interaction and human engagement

- Green workstyles were the analytical types, the ones who encouraged thoughtful analysis before action

Coming into the quiz, I was absolutely certain that I was going to be a strong Red. Up to that point and time, I had been a natural leader in most activities I participated in. I ran extracurricular groups, took charge of group projects, even worked a part-time job leading campus student groups. I filled the test out quickly and almost blithely, thinking to myself it was a silly exercise.

Imagine my surprise when the scores came back and I wasn't a Red, not really. Somehow, my scores for the assessment had placed me smack dab in the center triangle of the Venn Diagram of the personality types.

"Ah, you're a Hub!" said the testing coordinator when she handed me my results.

"A what?" I asked.

"A Hub." She smiled. "They don't actually align with any one workstyle type. Instead, we find that they usually assess group dynamics early on and then mold themselves to fill the gaps. So if a team has a lot of strong leaders and analytical thinkers, the Hub will take on the Blue role of bringing the human element to the conversation. They help round out teams."

"Huh. Sure, thanks." I took my results and I gave them a cursory glance before shoving them into my folder. I knew I wasn't a Hub. I was a Red.

But the more I thought about it, the more I realized it was true. I'd taken the lead on so many projects because there hadn't *been* a strong leader. At the same time, when working at one of the university offices, I often contributed from a place of empathy and compassion. There were plenty of leaders and analytical thinkers; those bases were covered. I could even pinpoint situations when I had shifted to the analytical mindset, asking for more data and information before sharing my thoughts on a topic.

As cliché as it is to say, that quiz changed my perspective on the role I played on teams far into the future. Even ten years later, I feel myself shifting roles and smile. Knowing and understanding my strengths on a team has helped me be a better team member, collaborator, and even individual worker.

As you begin your journey to build a better world, spend some time reflecting on your personal strengths and experiences. What role do you usually play in teams? What do you usually bring to a group setting? Keep your collaboration style in mind as you begin connecting with others to build a team, and work to understand the styles of your teammates. Building a diverse team of people with different perspectives, opinions, and working types can help your final solution succeed. As world-famous fashion designer Donatella Versace once said, "Creativity comes from a conflict of ideas."

HIDDEN SKILLS AND STRENGTHS

Knowing what one brings to a team goes beyond working type—it includes skills as well! You would be surprised what skills you have or what tools you're comfortable using that are completely unknown to others. As someone with a background in journalism, I was surprised when I began working in government that my colleagues were uncomfortable with graphic design and didn't know how to use tools that I thought were commonplace. I volunteered to help with work related to those needs, and as I collaborated with the team to apply those skills, I found myself playing a key role in our work.

Now that I work as a senior manager at a technology company, I'm delighted when a member of my team raises their hand to say, "I know that tool a bit; I used it at my internship." Even skills that are dormant or infrequently used can make a huge difference on a team, particularly a small one.

The same goes for your personal and professional experiences as well. Many times, we discount our own experiences because there is always someone else out there who has more experience or is more of an expert than we are. Even if that's the case, there is no one else in the world who has your exact same blend of skills, interests, and experiences. That unique blend of perspectives and talents can help make you an essential member of any team and help you find creative ways to solve problems that others may not have thought of before.

The next time you are introduced to a new group or team, make a mental note of the tools and experiences you bring to the table, and be sure to share them with your teammate. Encourage other members of your team to reflect on their "hidden talents" too. You never know what talents, working styles, or experiences will make all the difference.

FINDING YOUR TEAM

How and where you find your team will depend on your personal situation. Are you a student or an entrepreneur? Are you an employee at a nonprofit or well-established company? Are you an executive? We'll discuss in detail how to find your team in the Blueprints section of the book, with specific recommendations for the group you align most with.

In the meantime, as you continue reading, I encourage you to think of people you know who you'd like to collaborate with, or the type of people who you may need to collaborate with to begin your efforts. Dr. Freudenthal sought out the talents and traditions of local weavers to help save the children of La Paz. Tyler Hayes surrounds himself with people of different backgrounds and skill sets. The tech titans we discussed have changed the world by identifying gaps in their teams and finding people to fill them.

You may not know engineers or computer scientists or start-up founders, and that's okay. Those types of people are out there, and many of them are interested in making a difference. Even if there's not currently someone in your network who you can leverage to help get your idea off of the ground, don't be afraid to reach out to people through social media, shared connections, or experts you find through open-source research.

Are you feeling alone? If you need a team, consider me member number two. You can always reach me at www.techtosavetheworld.com, and I'll do everything I can to help you get started.

Let's get to work.

5

LISTENING AND LEARNING

WELL, WELL, WELL

Despite all of our technological progress, water still isn't a reliable resource around the world. In some countries, women walk for more than two hours a day to collect safe drinking water and bring it back to their families. Interestingly, the "water problem" has been solved a dozen times over by a wide range of technology tools.

- Water filtration systems draw water out of the earth to create artificial wells.
- Solar-powered systems draw moisture out of the atmosphere and create water out of thin air.
- Chemical tablets can be mixed into dirty water to make it usable.
- Desalination systems can take undrinkable ocean water and make it drinkable.

And yet, hundreds of thousands of people around the world still don't have access to reliable water sources.

Why?

Because the bulk of the potable water solutions are unrealistic for the communities that need the water most.

- They are exorbitantly expensive. (Imagine telling a village with a GDP equivalent of two hundred fifty dollars per year that a seventy-five-hundred-dollar water system will solve their problems.)
- They need people with specific skill sets to continue working. (If a water collection system has an electrical component that needs maintenance and upkeep, it will need ongoing care from an electrician or an engineer.)
- The solutions are unrealistic for the region. (How is a water production system going to collect moisture from a desert atmosphere?)

Take, for example, the infamous story of the PlayPump innovation, which was lauded in the early 2000s as a promising technology solution to water insecurity in Africa. It was a joyful premise. The PlayPump was designed in such a way that children would play on a merry-go-round that was installed to a water pump. Powered by the children's play, the pump would draw and store water in a storage tank that could be accessed on demand by locals.

It was a heartwarming and inspiring story that attracted worldwide acclaim and investment. Laura Bush, the First Lady of the United States at the time, pledged 16.4 million dollars in financial support. As media coverage and successful fundraising began to snowball, PlayPump went from a niche idea to a worldwide inspiration. Soon, PlayPumps were being installed in ten African nations. The pumps were initially lauded as a success; children enjoyed playing on the newly installed merry-go-rounds, and international media spread the good news.

As time passed, other causes drew away reporters and donors. PlayPump faded from the spotlight and was considered a general success. But something was wrong.

One of the first reporters to write about the PlayPump, a Frontline reporter named Amy Costello, returned to one of the PlayPump sites in Mozambique. She'd heard that something had been going wrong with them and wanted to see for herself what was going on.

When she arrived, she found broken and abandoned PlayPumps left and right. School officials told her the pumps installed at school sites often just stopped working or stopped storing water. Locals shared that after the children got bored of the merry-go-round, women would spend countless hours trying to spin the merry-go-rounds by hand.

The women shared that the PlayPumps frequently stopped working, and their calls and messages to PlayPump International to request repairs never received replies. A report by UNICEF later revealed that the PlayPumps would break down within as few as six weeks from being installed and be left without repair. Those that were repaired were often fixed after a wait of three months or more, at which point the locals distrusted using the pumps at all.

There weren't enough supplies to repair the PlayPumps that had been installed throughout Africa, and there didn't seem to be enough skilled laborers to conduct those repairs.

Worst of all, the women told Costello they hadn't been asked or informed about the PlayPumps being installed at the water pump site. They just arrived one day, without input or insight from the local community. If the locals had been asked, they would have shared that they were used to pumping water by hand (even if it wasn't ideal), and the local children would likely grow bored with a merry-go-round within a few weeks. They could have also helped assessors decide whether the sites had the right conditions for pumping large amounts of water.

This story—one of thousands—encapsulates one of the challenges with idealistic innovation. While we can build and share any number of technological advances, if we don't work with the people who would need to use them day-to-day to create and test them, we'll never solve the deeper problems.

START WITH THE EXPERTS

If you're working to design or build a new solution that will need to be used by a certain group of people, or will impact those people, you should begin talking to them as soon as possible. They know the ins and outs of the problem better than anyone else. They can share insights and nuances of the challenge. Even better, they usually know what's already been tried, what hasn't worked, and why.

By engaging with them early on, you can share initial ideas with them and then continue to gather their feedback on prototypes or early efforts. The feedback they share at each iteration loop will help you refine your solution until you've created something that truly addresses the problem.

An amazing example of this principle is the work of a then-college student, Tyler Skluzacek. Tyler's father, Patrick Skluzacek, was a veteran who returned from serving in Iraq in 2007 with severe PTSD. Patrick was plagued by traumatic nightmares that kept him from sleeping; when he closed his eyes, he found himself back on the battlefield. The lack of sleep made him prone to anger and mood swings, and he became so desperate that his only relief from the constant night battles were pills and alcohol.

Despite his attempts to get back on track, Patrick's life began to fall apart around him. His marriage collapsed, he lost his job, and he even lost his home. "He went off to do a twelve-month deployment as an energetic and generally happy guy. When he came back, he was pretty shaken up. It's one of those things where it's strange…with PTSD, you never notice it at first. We were just excited to have him home. But then a few weeks or months passed and the shine wore off. All of a sudden we noticed, 'Oh my god, something's not okay,'" shared Tyler.

Eight years later, Tyler was a college student studying computer science when he spotted a call for participants in a hackathon to create solutions for PTSD in collaboration with the Departments of Veterans Affairs and the Department of

Defense. He saved up his money to buy a cross-country plane ticket from his college in Minnesota to Washington, DC.

At the hackathon, Tyler and his team leaned heavily upon the expertise of the clinicians—many of whom were experts in the treatment of PTSD—as they began to brainstorm ways to use mobile technologies to help people who suffer from PTSD. One of the treatments that stuck with the team was the use of service dogs, who are trained to notice when their owner was having a nightmare and gently wake them up. The team set to work on building an app that could use smart-watch technology that measured heartbeat and movement to sense when a wearer was drifting into a nightmare and use an intelligent buzz to draw the person out of the nightmare without fully waking them.

By the end of the hackathon, the group had a winning proto-type solution, but no way to test it. So Tyler went to someone he knew could benefit from the app.

"I got to bring it back home to my dad. I said, 'Hey, Dad, I had this idea and we coded up this application, do you want to try it?'"

Patrick immediately burst into tears and said, "I'm willing to try anything to sleep."

Tyler and Patrick began testing the application with Tyler reviewing each night's collected data and iterating on the application's sensing and vibration capabilities. Patrick would talk through each night's experience and share ideas for improvement.

"He wore a lot of bad versions of the watch, which I guess comes with being a guinea pig," chuckled Tyler. "But really, over two to three months, it started working fantastically well."

Tyler shared the success with his hackathon team and the clinicians who had advised him during the event and beyond. In 2020, the application rebranded as NightWare was approved by the Food and Drug Administration as a prescription available treatment for sufferers of PTSD. Tyler's collaboration with his father—someone who understood PTSD and traumatic nightmares intimately—resulted in a potentially lifesaving solution for veterans and others around the world.

PEOPLE WHO UNDERSTAND THE PROBLEM HAVE GREAT SOLUTIONS

The more people you talk with to understand a problem or an opportunity, the more you'll learn about the flavor and nuance of the challenge. And the more people you consult with along the way, the more options you'll have to solve it. People who deal with the problem firsthand may even share simple, powerful ideas that require no technology at all.

When working as a technology consultant, one of my jobs was to recommend ways an office could improve their communication and "break down siloes." The long-term goal was to find a new software that would solve the problem. Part of my job was to interview different members of the office at all levels.

If you're thinking, *That just sounds like listening to people with extra steps*, you're exactly right.

For the next three months, my job was to talk to people. I had a set list of interview questions that my boss recommended I ask, but I would also go off script and dig into certain topics if the person I was meeting with seemed particularly passionate about them. And my goodness, did they talk. Nearly every interview I held went over time. The people I met with were excited to share their perspectives and talk about their work and their challenges.

During that time, my colleagues and I interviewed seventy-five people and collected more than two hundred fifty survey responses, all from people providing insight into the biggest challenges they faced in their workplace.

I think you can guess what we found.

People in the office just didn't talk to each other.

That was it. That was the core takeaway of our report. The issue wasn't technology, it was the people culture. Our clients were overworked, overlooked, and didn't feel as though they had support from their leadership to make decisions and push work forward. So, they didn't.

When we delivered our recommendations, we presented them to an open forum of the office's employees. We walked through our findings one by one to a group of more than thirty people who took time out of their day to learn what we had found. When we shared our number one recommendation—weekly meetings with leadership for each team—one of the executives stopped our presentation.

"I thought that you were supposed to figure out which technology tool would help us communicate better," she said.

"We were," I replied. "But we don't think you need it. We recommend that you try these simple recommendations first and see if they solve your problem. If it doesn't, we can use the same information we already collected to help you find a technology solution."

The weekly meeting recommendation had been suggested to us by one of the employees we interviewed. It was the simplest answer. As a consultant, I felt almost silly giving it. But when they began implementing it, their communication significantly improved. If we hadn't interviewed the employees and asked them for ideas, we might have focused on more complicated and expensive solutions.

LISTENING IS LEARNING

Talking to other people—especially people who have intimate experience with the problem we're hoping to solve—is one of the most powerful tools available to us. We can learn from them, we can better empathize with them, and we can better understand their needs and challenges. When you begin working on your own idealistic innovation, carve out time for you and your team to meet with users, locals, and experts in the field. Ask lots of questions. Ask for their advice, their ideas, and their feedback. Most people will be happy to share their perspective with you.

Listen, learn, and weave what you've learned into your project. Your innovation will be more successful and more impactful because of it.

6

ITERATING

—

FACING A VERY HUMAN FEAR

"Failure is not an option" is such a famous quote from the film *Apollo 13* that it is still repeated on T-shirts and coffee mugs, by sports teams, in classrooms, and even in business meetings more than twenty-five years after the film's release.

There's something about that quip, almost a throwaway line, that still resonates with us today. People not only hate failure, but we often fear it. Failure is seen as something to be avoided at nearly any cost. After all, we often believe that failure reflects negatively on us.

"At the root of failure and the fear of failure is shame, which is a very unpleasant emotion associated with feeling like one is a bad person, or has a flawed or defective self," says Taya Cohen, Associate Professor of Organizational Behavior and Theory at Carnegie Mellon University's Tepper School of Business.

To our credit, fear of failure is understandable in a world where we're taught that to fail is to hit rock bottom, to prevent ourselves from achieving our goals. From our education system to our interpersonal relationships to our careers, we've learned throughout our lives that to fail is to cause irreversible harm to ourselves, to the people around us, and to our futures.

"Failure is a feeling long before it becomes an actual result. It's vulnerability that breeds with self-doubt and then is escalated, often deliberately, by fear," writes Michelle Obama in her book *Becoming*.

Unfortunately, this fear of failure holds us back and limits our creativity. Instead of venturing into the unknown or trying something new, even related to the things we're passionate about, many of us stay "within our lanes" and within our comfort zones. Even while reading this book, you may have found yourself thinking, *I'd like to try that, but there's no way I'd succeed.*

Humans don't like to fail, especially not when something important is at stake. I've worked with many clients who wanted to scrap a project after weeks of work because they weren't seeing the exact results they were looking for. What they didn't understand is that application of technology to nearly any problem is a learning process. Very rarely can even the most put-together team identify and account for any and all challenges, requirements, and situations that need to be considered for the technology to be successful.

What if we turned the concept of failure on its head? What if instead of something to be feared, failure became something to celebrate? IBM's former chairman and CEO Thomas J. Watson once said, "You are thinking of failure as the enemy of success. But it isn't at all. You can be discouraged by failure, or you can learn from it. So go ahead and make mistakes. Make all you can. Because remember that's where you will find success."

That seems a bit counterintuitive, doesn't it? How can failure lead to greater success down the road?

EMBRACING FAILURE TO FIND SUCCESS

"If you're not prepared to fail, you're not prepared to learn," writes Bill Taylor, cofounder of *Fast Company* and the author of *Simply Brilliant: How Great Organizations Do Ordinary Things in Extraordinary Ways.* "Unless people…keep learning as fast as the world is changing, they'll never keep growing and evolving."

Failure is one of life's most memorable teachers. Take a moment to reflect on your life up to this point. How many major successes do you remember? Now, how many critical failures come to mind? What did you learn from those successes, and those failures? For many people, their many failures along the winding road of life have taught them how to change what they do to have better outcomes in the future.

That same lesson can be applied to our efforts in idealistic innovation in the form of iteration. Projects and efforts are more successful when we iterate upon them: starting something, testing it, tweaking it based on feedback, and testing it again.

"At its heart, innovation is based on the scientific method," writes Ron Ashkenas, coauthor of the *Harvard Business Review Leader's Handbook*. "Develop a hypothesis, test it, and find out if it's valid. Doing this well requires repeated failures. But each one helps you cross out one more invalid hypothesis and gets you closer to figuring out what will really work."

One of the most well-known iterators in history, Thomas Edison, attributed his success to his ability to embrace and learn from what others might consider failure. He and his team tested *more than three thousand prototypes* of lightbulbs over the course of three years before filing for his famous patent in 1879. "If I find ten thousand ways something won't work, I haven't failed," said Edison. "I am not discouraged because every wrong attempt discarded is often a step forward."

EDGE INNOVATION DOLPHIN AND THE SPIRIT OF ITERATION

The dolphin cut the surface of the water with its fin as it glided across the shallow pool. Across the way, a little girl giggled, waving her hand at the creature. The dolphin spotted her, and with a fluid swish of its tail, it swam to the edge of the pool to her. The girl squealed in delight and excitement, reaching out to touch the snout lifted toward her. "Oh, honey, no, we can't touch," her mother said, and began to pull her away.

"No, she's okay!" The dolphin's attendant waved from a few feet away. He walked over and extended his hand, gently placing it on the dolphin's snout. "She can touch it. See?" He smiled to the parents as the father leaned forward and the baby ran her hands over the dolphin's smooth skin. The dolphin squeaked and wiggled, splashing a bit of water with its tail.

"Are you sure?" the mother asked. "Is it safe?"

"Oh, yes. This is a robotic dolphin," the handler replied with a smile.

Edge Innovations' creation of an animatronic dolphin, a technology triumph that has the potential to change how we engage with marine mammals, is a modern-day tale of iteration. To the naked eye, the life-sized, ultra-realistic robot is as good as the real thing. It can swim freely, interact, and make eye contact. It can be set to swim naturally in "exhibit" mode or switched over to a remote-control mode for interactions with animal lovers. It looks, moves, breathes, acts, and feels like a live dolphin. In pilots to test whether the robot could be as educational and entertaining as the real thing, attendees thought they were interacting with a living, breathing animal. "When I first saw the dolphin, I thought it could be real. It even *felt* like a real dolphin."

The robots are similar in size to their living counterparts and can be stored in freshwater or saltwater, which is a notoriously tricky feat of engineering. As robots, their life-support systems are simple; they just need to be plugged in overnight to recharge. Their batteries can last up to ten hours. In addition to being a more humane option for human-animal interactions, they can perform for and interact with people without concerns of potential behavioral and safety issues.

While researching the dolphins and the ways they could be used—education, entertainment, conservation, field research—I met with the men who had brought the robot to life, Edge Innovations CEO Walt Conti and former Vice President/Creative Director at Walt Disney Imagineering Roger Holzberg. When I asked them how long it took them to build, I was surprised to discover that the animatronic dolphin was *twenty years* in the making. That's right; the original concept to replace live animals at marine parks with animatronic robots was tested at Walt Disney World and the Disney company's private island, Castaway Cay, in the early 2000s.

The inspiration for the project was born when Walt and his team were leading special effects and animatronic puppeteering for the films *Free Willy* and *Flipper.* "On the set between takes, we would play around with the joysticks and keep the [animatronic] interaction going," shared Walt, who was the designer puppeteer for the animatronics. "The actors would keep engaging and talking to the animals. It was this weird suspension of disbelief. These actors normally would go off to their trailers, but instead they were hanging out, touching the orca's flippers. It wasn't just to get a laugh; they would do it continuously, basically hanging out with a machine and a piece of rubber because of that illusion of realism. They were connecting not intellectually, but emotionally."

That emotional connection led Roger, who was an Imagineering Creative Director overseeing the EPCOT portfolio, to reach out to Walt in hopes of collaborating on a lifelike dolphin animatronic for theme park attractions. The vision was to combine Edge Innovations' special effects and puppetry with more robust controls to enable real-time interaction.

"I reached out to Walt with the idea of creating an up-close, very personal experience," said Roger. "For the first time in history, it would be something interactive as opposed to a preprogrammed, scripted animatronic show. It would be a free-swimming, free-ranging figure. We could learn about the world's oceans from the point of view of someone who actually lived there. We did a pilot, which tested higher than almost any attraction Imagineering had ever done up to that point."

While the pilot was a triumph, it was poorly timed. Disney executives were unsure of how to scale the initiative, offering it to broader groups of park and cruise ship guests. After acquiring Pixar, Disney shifted the focus of its oceanic themed attractions at Walt Disney World to align with the popular film *Finding Nemo.* The robotic dolphin, despite being a huge success, was shelved.

Years later, in 2018, Walt and Roger were contacted by Chinese marine mammal park investors who were shocked when they began to budget for their new, multi-oceanarium initiative that would include dozens of marine mammals of multiple species. The price tag and growing negative sentiments around captive whales and dolphins drove them to consider the use of robots instead of live animals in the parks. When they began researching ideas and found videos of the early Disney tests online, they reached out to Roger and Walt.

"My initial response was 'No, I don't do this anymore,'" shared Roger, who had gone on to found a health care technology company. "But my wife said, 'If you come together and partner with Walt on this and keep three large aquariums from capturing sixty or eighty large marine mammals from the world's oceans, you'll have changed the history of those species.'"

Luckily for them, technology had come a long way in the years that had passed.

Since the early 2000s, critical advancements had been made in sensors, lithium batteries, and processing by electronic companies like Apple and in the electric vehicle industry. While the previous dolphin prototypes had tethers connected to control panels that provided power and allowed the team to control the robot, the newer iteration could be powered by lithium batteries and swim autonomously. In fact, batteries had progressed so far that the team realized they could use lithium batteries to power an orca-sized animatronic. "We're riding tens of billions of dollars of technology investment in those industries," said Walt.

Beyond the technology leaps forward, the modern version of the robotic dolphin has been iterated upon at each step to find new improvements and solutions. "There have been levels of evolution," said Walt.

The first prototype was a puppeteer animatronic that had to be remotely controlled, similar to the ones used for prior movie sets. In recent years, the team has been able to add features that make the dolphin more lifelike. They've incorporated onboard intelligence features, including buoyancy control and natural behaviors like surfacing for breath. The team is currently working on a version 3.0 of the dolphin, which will be fully autonomous and behave like a natural dolphin until the remote-control mode is turned on for entertainment or educational shows. At every step of the way, the development team tested new features, iterating, tweaking, and adjusting to get the robotic dolphin just right.

Edge Innovations, which had previously developed animatronics for famous films, including *Free Willy, Anaconda,* and *Deep Blue Sea,* hopes to expand the use of this technology and the techniques they've learned through iteration to create other species. Initial prototype ideas include Jurassic-era aquatic dinosaurs, water dragons, and great white sharks.

While it's an incredible story of iteration, Walt and Roger's story is also one of persistence and reinvigoration. They developed a functional realistic dolphin animatronic *twenty years ago,* and they have capitalized upon enhancements in technology to create a more lifelike, autonomous robot that could forever change conservation, education, and aquatic research.

EVERYDAY ITERATION

I loved chatting with Walt and Roger about their work because they reminded me very much of my father, Terry Nichols, who was a mechanic. After retiring from work as an Indy Racing Car pit crewman, he started his own small business fixing old cars that often seemed beyond repair. Calling himself "the Old Car Doctor," he would take in the mangiest and most rusted out pieces of junk I had ever seen and try to make them new again.

Many of the cars he worked on were so old that parts no longer existed for them. He couldn't go to an auto store and buy what he needed. Instead, he would have to create his own parts or customize others to make them fit. As a girl, I spent many summers being unwillingly dragged to his workshop. I would sit and read a book and sullenly roll my eyes as he hammered away, trying to customize a part to fit a car that, in my haughty teenage opinion, shouldn't be allowed to restart anyway.

Only through the lens of my adult years can I appreciate my father's hard work and why his business was so important to him. He breathed life back into old cars that had collector's value, but more importantly, he often repaired vehicles that had a deeply sentimental meaning to their owners. In some cases, it was a car they had dreamed about owning as a teenager but could only afford in their golden years. In others, he revived family heirlooms on wheels.

He did so by iterating. While I would sit in the corner of his shop, bored, with my nose buried in a book, I'd watch him out of the corner of my eye as he would tinker with a part, put it in the car, start the car to test it, and take the part back out again to tinker some more. He shaped, drilled, ground, rebuilt, and duct taped countless pieces of equipment together, doing whatever he could to bring the old cars back to life.

And every time, he succeeded. Sometimes it would take him just a few days to get a car running, other projects took him years. He even spent years repairing the iconic truck from the cult classic film *Hoosiers,* which can be seen running today at festivals and parades in Indianapolis, Indiana, and Washington, DC.

My dad's work showed me how there are just some projects and tasks that you can't perfectly plan out. If he had tried to approach every repair from a "one size fits all" or had tried to map out every step he would need to take to get the car running again with no room for error, he likely would have failed time and time again. As it was, many of his projects ran long because he ran into challenges that he couldn't have predicted from the start.

Only his stubbornness, ingenuity, passion for the craft, and knack for iteration helped him through every time.

FAILING FORWARD

I mentioned previously that humans hate to fail. What's interesting is that every time we fail, we learn, we adapt, and many times we come back stronger. Because technology can feel so complicated and overwhelming, failures can feel catastrophic and are often viewed as something that must be avoided at all costs. What's important to remember is that no piece of technology you use today—computers, smartphones, video games, televisions—were perfect the first time. In fact, we've watched them continue to evolve and improve in real time over the course of our lifetimes.

Why should your innovations be any different?

7

LET'S GET TO WORK

—

NOW IS YOUR TIME

For much of human history, curiosity and the spirit of creativity have driven us to explore, to tinker, and to improve our day-to-day life. Throughout the centuries, we have charted a path from humble hunter-gatherers and cave dwellers to a long-living species with its eyes now turned toward the stars.

In 1969, Neil Armstrong was the first man to set foot on the moon. Fifty years later, we carry around a phone in our pocket with one hundred thousand times the processing power of the computer that got him there.

Most of us use that power to watch our favorite shows or share pictures of our pets. But we can use it for so much more.

We can use it to solve the problems that keep us awake at night, regardless of our personal, professional, or educational backgrounds. Technology is just a tool; what matters, and what will make a difference in our world, is how everyday people use it. Everyday people like you.

Now is the time. Now is your time.

CHOOSE YOUR OWN ADVENTURE

From here, *Tech to Save the World* becomes a workbook to building a better world. Of course, every reader is going to come in with different backgrounds, experiences, and expertise. That means some of the content in these guides may not be helpful to you.

If we're going to change the world, we'll be charting new paths. I invite you to use this section as a "choose your own adventure" guidebook. Make notes in the margins and dog-ear your favorite pages. If you begin reading and find yourself thinking, *I already know this*, jump ahead or skip the chapter altogether. You may find yourself jumping around the next two sections, and that's just fine.

THE WORKSHOP

The Workshop section is designed to help you build your own toolbox of skills, techniques, and technologies that you can use in your own passion projects.

In **Building Comfort with Technology,** we'll talk through how you can become more comfortable with tech and technology-related topics. We'll also explore why some people feel anxious about using technology and what can be done to overcome that.

In **Design Thinking—Dreaming to New Ideas,** we'll explore some of the brainstorming and problem-solving methods that are used in leading technology and consulting companies to address grand challenges.

In **(Some Of) The Tools of Innovation,** you'll find easy-to-understand explanations of increasingly popular technologies like drones, artificial intelligence, and the dreaded 5G.

THE BLUEPRINTS TO BUILDING A BETTER WORLD

The Blueprints section provides step-by-step examples of how idealistic innovation projects come to life. You only need to read the section that best aligns with your current scenario, but you're welcome to read through all three to see how innovation efforts can vary based on access to different skills, money, and information. While the characters and stories highlighted in these sections are fictitious, they are inspired by real-life idealistic innovation projects.

Blueprint for Dreamers

Dreamers are the readers who have limited access to resources (money, team members, support) but who still want to start making a difference in the world. Examples of dreamers include students, entrepreneurs, new nonprofit founders, and professionals who work in spaces that do not align with their world-changing goals.

Blueprint for Professionals

Professionals are the readers who currently work in a setting that allows them access to some resources (funding available for special projects, team member availability, job alignment to the goal). Professionals include people who work at nonprofit organizations, technology professionals working at companies that provide time or money for research and development, or people working at organizations that set aside funding for philanthropy or special projects.

Blueprint for Executives

Executives are leaders at companies and nonprofits who may not have the time to be in the "day-to-day" of idealistic innovation but who can assign funding, talent, time, and other resources toward a goal. The Executive Blueprint will be useful for nonprofit executives, private sector executives at technology companies with philanthropy goals, government officials, or high-ranking executives in other spaces who want to bring more innovation into their organization.

LET'S GET TO WORK

You should have nearly everything you need to get started, but if you want more information or support, you can always find me at www.techtosavetheworld.com. I'm happy to chat with you about your ideas, help you and your team brainstorm, connect you with experts, and help you work through the next steps whenever you get stuck.

You wouldn't have read *Tech to Save the World* if you didn't want to change the world.

So, in the words of *Parks and Recreation*'s famous government bureaucrat and role model Leslie Knope, "Theodore Roosevelt once said, *'Far and away the best prize that life offers is the chance to work hard at work worth doing...'* **We get the chance to work hard at work worth doing, alongside a team of people we love. Now, go find your team and get to work."**

THE WORKSHOP

8

BUILDING COMFORT WITH TECHNOLOGY

TECHNOLOGY CAN BE INTIMIDATING

Even though we use technology day in and day out, that doesn't mean it's a comfortable subject for everyone. For many it can be frightening, frustrating, and straight-up intimidating. It has had a significant impact on our lives from the time most of us were born; it has infiltrated and impacted our day-to-day lives in almost every sense.

Sure, technology can do great things, but if you get frustrated trying to log into your email, how can you possibly be one of those people who can use it to change the world?

"People tend to express the highest level of fear for things they're dependent on but that they don't have any control over, and that's almost a perfect definition of technology," says Christopher Bader, a professor of sociology at Chapman

University, who leads the university's study and annual Survey of American Fears.

"You can no longer make it in society without using technology…to buy things at a store, to talk to other people, to conduct business. People are increasingly dependent, but they don't have any idea how these things actually work."

Our reliance on day-to-day technologies can inspire any number of fears. The fear that we will break something we depend on. The fear that we are too stupid to use simple tools that everyone else seems to understand. The fear that our use of technology may come back to haunt us in the form of identity theft or an information hack. These feelings are natural and stem from a lack of control.

And of course, technology is constantly changing. It can feel as though as soon as we understand how to use Zoom or our favorite mobile phone app, an update is pushed through that moves everything around or keeps it from working altogether.

Unfortunately, you and I are never going to master all of the technology tools out there. By the time we'd learn them, they'd just change again.

The good news is that you *can* build your comfort level and master technology tools that help build a better world. In fact, you've likely already done it. During the COVID-19 pandemic, many businesses closed their physical locations and had their employees work from home using popular tech tools like laptops and Zoom.

Meanwhile, fewer people were traveling to see family and turned to social media and virtual holidays to fill the gap. Few of us knew what these tools were and how to use them, but we were forced to adopt them during the pandemic. If you were able to learn a new tool at the height of a globally stressful time, you can absolutely continue to do so.

You've done this once. You can do it again. Explore with an open mind and a kind heart toward yourself.

The best thing we can do to become more comfortable with it and more confident in our own skills is to work on developing what is known as a growth mindset.

CULTIVATING A GROWTH MINDSET TO INSPIRE INNOVATION

According to Stanford psychologist Carol Dweck, there are traditionally two styles of mindsets around our perceptions of our own intelligence and capabilities.

A **fixed mindset** is one in which we believe our traits are stable and unchangeable. People with fixed mindsets are more likely to view struggles or failures as a sign that they are incapable of success, or that they'll "just never get it."

A **growth mindset** is one in which we believe our traits are changeable and can be improved with effort, time, and support or guidance. "This growth mindset is based on the belief that your basic qualities are things you can cultivate through your efforts. Although people may differ in every which way in their initial talents and aptitudes, interests, or temperaments, everyone can change and grow through application and experience," says Dweck.

Of these two groups of people, those with fixed mindsets are more likely to avoid challenges, quit when they encounter an obstacle, and set smaller or more achievable personal and professional goals. Those who possess growth mindsets are more likely to try improving their capabilities and traits. Those with growth mindsets are also more likely to put in more effort when a challenge arises and set loftier goals. Even when they fall short of those goals, those with growth mindsets appreciate the time and energy they spent in pursuit of them.

Many of us have developed these mindsets throughout the course of our lives, frequently as a result of our own personal struggles, through observation of the people around us, and through societal cues and pressures. Regardless of which mindset you have right now, the good news is that they can be shifted over time.

THOUGHT EXERCISE: TECHNOLOGY FEARS

If you are one of those people who feels as though they don't understand technology, I'd like you to do a quick mental exercise with me.

- When you think about technology and you feel the uncertainty rise, what are the thoughts connected to the sensation?

- Is it a feeling of being overwhelmed or anxious?
- Is it a frustration based on your previous technology experiences?
- Is it doubt?

The way to overcome this sensation of "not being a tech person" is different for everyone, based on the root of your own personal views and perspectives. Inspired by my career of working with people from all walks of life, I offer a few suggestions to cultivate a growth mindset around working with technology and prove to yourself that you are a tech person.

EXERCISE TO BUILD COMFORT #1:
GETTING TO KNOW YOUR FAVORITE TECH

For those who feel uncertainty, perhaps you're doubting yourself. I would argue that anyone can "get" technology if they're interested in learning more about it. Try to identify a technology you enjoy or know well and give yourself just thirty minutes to learn more about it.

As an example, while writing this sentence, Siri (my iPhone's artificial intelligence driven personal assistant) began reading a text message my mom sent to me. I've always used Siri as my personal assistant and I'm very fond of him. If I'm feeling uncertain about my ability to understand complex technologies, I might do some quick googling on Siri and how he was made. That would quickly lead me to information about artificial intelligence, voice recognition, and natural language processing.

While reading, I would likely encounter terms and references that I wouldn't understand. I'd research those as I went, too, taking notes for myself. Within thirty minutes, I'd have a much stronger understanding of how and why Siri works. That knowledge could be beneficial to me as I was thinking of creative ways to solve challenges in the future. Even better, having that understanding would give me confidence in my ability to build future knowledge.

EXERCISE TO BUILD COMFORT #2: EXPLORING INTERESTING TECHNOLOGY USES

For those who feel overwhelmed, first take a deep breath. This sensation is a personal one to me and I know it well. I have to fight against it every day, even though I work in the technology field! If you're interested in learning more about technology or want to try to use tech to solve for a problem, start small.

We've already discussed how most technologies require a wide range of skills to be made and successfully used. Remember that you don't need to know everything about a particular technology to make it work for you.

Instead of looking for information about a specific technology, explore technology around a topic you're comfortable with. Do you love whales? Do a quick search on marine mammal conservation technology. Do a deep dive on how researchers and conservationists are using different tech tools from drones to artificial intelligence to study whales and help them thrive.

When you come across a term you don't understand, be kind to yourself and look it up. If you hit a point where you're losing interest, take a break or move on to another technology tool. You don't need to be an expert. Having a basic understanding of what tools are available and how they can work together is your head start to changing the world.

IT'S OKAY TO BE A SKEPTIC

If you're feeling doubt in yourself or in tech's ability to make an impact, perhaps you've been let down by technology before, or you've seen expensive projects fail time and time again. This can actually be a great thing.

You have a clearer picture of how technology development works (or fails), and you'll be better able to navigate the twists and turns ahead. You'll also likely stay focused on solving the *problem* rather than trying to shoehorn a technology solution that may not be the best option. In my opinion, if you're feeling a bit of doubt, you're ahead of the game.

9

DESIGN THINKING— DREAMING TO BIG IDEAS

WHAT IS DESIGN THINKING?

Almost anyone you ask will agree that yes, of course, they'd like to change the world. The things they'd like to change may vary from politics to animal conservation to climate change, but everyone cares about *something* enough to do something about it.

But do what, exactly?

There's often a disconnect between enthusiasm and execution. Even someone who is wildly passionate about saving the rainforests, for instance, may have no idea of where or how to start. If you're reading this book, it's likely that you have an idea of a problem you'd like to help solve, but you're not sure what to do about it. Where do all of those big, innovative, world-changing ideas come from?

While inspiration can come from anywhere—corporate retreats, fever dreams, a superhero movie montage—I recommend starting from scratch and imagining new solutions using Design Thinking tools. *Harvard Business Review* explains that Design Thinking is "a methodology that imbues the full spectrum of innovation activities with a human-centered design ethos."

For those of us outside of the boardroom, this means true innovation is driven by a clear understanding of the problem being solved for with the end users in mind. That understanding can only come through communication, collaboration, and viewing the problem from a variety of angles. While formal Design Thinking aligns with a series of structured phases, including inspiration, ideation, and implementation, you can pick and choose pieces that work best for your team to dig deeper into opportunities for using technology to make a difference.

Lou Lenzi, a Professor of Human-Computer Interaction at Indiana University and one of the top fifty industrial designers over the last fifty years, relied on Design Thinking concepts throughout his former career as an industrial design senior executive at companies like IBM, General Electric, and RCA. "You can call it Design Thinking, human-centered design, or user study. Understand and frame the problem correctly, use an iterative design process to continually refine that product or service you're building, and use the technology to your benefit."

While Design Thinking sounds like a fancy corporate methodology, many exercises are actually quite simple. To use them, you just need:

- A whiteboard (real or virtual)
- Some sticky notes
- Preferably, a team of other people to bounce ideas off of

I won't comprehensively cover the world of Design Thinking methodologies in this book; there are a number of other excellent resources available online or in print. But as you embark on your journey to be the change you want to see in the world through technology, here are some of the most accessible Design Thinking exercises you can use to come up with and test your ideas.

UNDERSTANDING THE PROBLEM

FIVE (TO NINE) WHYS

Five Whys, sometimes known as Nine Whys, is an exercise that asks the team to dig deep beneath their assumptions and share their understanding of the root of a problem.

As an example, let's imagine you and your team are interested in saving the whales; specifically, killer whales, certain types of which are endangered. Your Five Whys conversation may go something like this:

Team Member 1: "It's really sad. Growing up, I used to see whales all the time, but I haven't seen one in the wild in a long time."

Team Member 2: **"Why?"**

Team Member 1: "According to NOAA, in recent decades, several populations of killer whales have declined and some have even become endangered."

Team Member: **"Why?"**

Team Member 1: "One reason is chemical contamination. Apparently, pesticides, wastewater, and other contaminants make their way into the ocean, which trickle upward to the killer whales."

Team Member 2: **"Why?"**

Team Member 3: "Killer whales are at the top of the food chain. Other sea life eats or absorbs those contaminants, and in turn whales ingest them when they eat that sea life. Some of the chemicals can be especially harmful to whales because of their extended life span and blubber stores. In some cases, when dead whales wash up on shore, they are so contaminated that they are considered toxic waste."

Team Member 2: **"Why do the contaminants wind up in the water in the first place?"**

Team Member 3: "Some of the most dangerous, PCB chemicals, have been in use since the 1930s. Even though they have been banned, 80 percent of the one million tons produced have not been destroyed and are still leaking into seas from landfills and other locations."

Team Member 2: **"Why?"**

Team Member 1: "PCB is inconvenient and expensive to clean up and dispose of. While some countries, like the United States, have launched dedicated efforts to clean contaminated areas of PCB, most countries around the world have instead banned further use of them in hopes that their impact fades over time."

In this case, your group may decide to explore technology applications to cleaning up PCB as a way to help preserve the remaining population of killer whales.

The trick with Five to Nine Whys is that you may hit a point where your knowledge (or your team's knowledge) is limited. While the exercise is traditionally done in a round robin or group setting, be willing to take some time to pause and research.

Once you've identified some select root causes to explore, you should try to focus whatever solution you and your team create around addressing those root causes directly. Many would-be idealistic innovations fail because they target the symptoms of problems rather than the root issues, limiting their impact on the broader challenge. As you move forward, look back at your Five Whys frequently to keep them at the heart of your efforts.

HOW MIGHT WE

Taking challenges and turning them into opportunities is empowering. Instead of looking at the problem you're trying to solve for as a Big Problem, using the phrase "How Might

We…" when thinking of solutions offers the team the ability to creatively share solutions.

To run a How Might We exercise, take a look at some of the problems you've defined. Take them, one at a time, and ask the team, "How might we XYZ?"

As an example, let's say that your team is working on preserving coral reefs. Through research and interviews, you learned that some reefs around the world are destroyed by blast fishing. Many village fishermen around the world use dynamite or other explosives to stun or kill fish and collect them when they float to the top.

The team conducted a deeper dive on this issue, exploring the problem through Five Whys. You determined that blast fishing is popular because fishermen are able to kill and collect far more fish using less energy and time than would be needed for other traditional fishing methods.

To begin the exercise, you could write on the team's whiteboard, "How Might We Make Blast Fishing Less Desirable?" The team could then discuss options; perhaps making blast fishing illegal? Issuing fines? Creating a tool that could provide stronger oversight in locations where it's already illegal? Developing some method to scare away fish from the reef when boats approach?

You can also approach the question from a positive angle, like "How Might We Make Other Types of Fishing Easier for the Fishermen?"

Another method of becoming more familiar with a problem is interviewing people who experience that challenge directly, or people who have conducted significant research to understand the root causes of the problem. As an example, if you were looking to find ways to ease homelessness, you might interview people experiencing homelessness to hear about their experiences directly. You might also reach out to researchers, government officials, or university scholars who have spoken or published about ways to improve homelessness in their community and around the world.

To run an effective interview:

- Be respectful. Unless you're offering an incentive to meet with you, you are borrowing someone's time. Thank them for meeting with you and sharing their perspective.
- Do some research beforehand. Come prepared with a perspective on the subject, but also be ready to listen and learn.
- Have a list of questions ready. Be clear on what type of information you would like to get from the interview. If you're not getting the information you were hoping for, be flexible and try changing up the types of questions you are asking.
- If you are able to, record the audio of the interview. While you should still take notes during the discussion, having a recording will allow you to focus on the conversation rather than capturing everything being shared. If you're unable to record, bring a teammate to help you take notes. Be sure to ask permission to record the conversation.

- Listen closely to responses to your questions and be willing to go off script to ask follow-up questions, ask for more details, or ask questions that arise from previously shared answers.
- Use strategic silence to get more detailed answers. Many people are predisposed to dislike silence and awkward pauses and will rush to fill the void. In my experience, information shared at that point in an interview is often candid and insightful.
- Ask for ideas! People close to the problems often have excellent ideas for how to solve them, but sometimes lack the resources or the know-how. Some of your best solution options may come from the people you interview.

Meeting with direct stakeholders or people who are familiar with the challenge you are trying to solve will provide you with more insight into the issue that you likely hadn't encountered before. It will also give you an opportunity to pulse ideas with people who are experienced in the space, and to brainstorm with them directly.

Professor Lenzi emphasizes the power of connecting with users early on. "People who understand the frontline user and understand the user experience can design for that end user; their pains, their gains, what they're trying to accomplish. They can create value propositions that are more in tune to the user, which will be more successful."

As a consultant, some of the best ideas I have implemented in the business world were suggested by existing employees who I interviewed about the problem. They were closest to the challenge, they knew what had been done before, and they had new perspectives on how to bring change.

CREATING SOLUTIONS

GO IT ALONE (AT THE START)

After you and your team have defined the problem you'd like to try to help solve, take a bit of a break from the group work. Clearly outline the problem and prompt every member of the team to spend some time over the next few days thinking of ideas on their own. Ask every member of the team, regardless of their role, to come back to the group with three to five ideas of how to solve the problem. This gives everyone some time and mental space to think about the problem rather than focus on sharing ideas immediately after it's been defined.

The next time the group gets together, have everyone write out a brief description of their ideas and share them with the group. See how these ideas resonate with the group. Are people particularly excited about a few options? Do other ideas kind of fall to the wayside? Use this to narrow down your list of ideas for initial discussion.

Once your group has all of the ideas outlined and the weaker ideas have been set aside, ask people to share more detail about their ideas. Have the other members of the team ask questions, share feedback, and build on the initial concepts through discussion.

After you've talked through the top ideas, pause and ask the group which ones sparked the most interest and seemed most realistic given your team's skill sets. Your team will likely gravitate toward two or three to explore further, research, and even prototype.

YES AND

"Yes And" is an ideation exercise where teammates always agree with what their teammate has previously said, and then build upon the idea with something new. The exercise is built around the idea that criticizing or ignoring initial ideas can limit a group's creativity and box them into traditional ways of thinking. While some of the outcomes of "Yes And" can seem silly and nonsensical, you and your team may be surprised at the ideas you can collaboratively create.

To run "Yes And," one team member should start with the bones of an idea, even a silly one. As an example, let's say the team was working to address world hunger:

Team Member 1: "We could teach everyone in the world to cook. We could make a global cooking phone app."

Team Member 2: "Yes, and the app could also show people how to grow some of their own food—vegetables, crops— to cook."

Team Member 3: "Yes, and we could even have the app use location data to determine what types of crops would be easiest to grow so they'd have a higher likelihood of success."

Team Member 4: "Yes, and we could even include instructions on how to care for each plant/crop, and fixes for common agricultural issues."

Once you've determined which root problem you'd like to solve for, and you have a few solution ideas from "Yes And" or "How Might We," it's time to bring your vision to life!

Ten-Minute Prototypes let you and your team quickly create a first version of whatever solution you're hoping to explore. It can take many forms—it can be a storyboard, a paper drawing, a play-dough sculpture, or a cardboard mock-up. The prototype doesn't need to actually *work*; it just needs to offer you a way to visualize it and consider the solution from new angles.

After you've pulled together your prototype, walk through the story of it with the team—the problem it solves, what it does, how it's used. Ask critical questions about the mock up.

Can it actually help address the root cause of the problem?

What materials will be needed? Is it a realistic effort, given your team's skills?

If it needs to be used by someone, is it user-friendly? Does it meet their needs? How do you know?

Remember, the point of this effort is not to walk away with a working solution. It's intended to give you the opportunity to think more deeply about your idea!

From the time it opened its doors in 1874 until the mid 2010s, the Rotterdam Eye Hospital in the Netherlands was just what you might envision when you think of a hospital: grim, austere, and cold. Like most medical facilities, its appearance inspired anxiety and even fear in the patients who passed through its doors.

When the hospital's board of directors learned that most patients who passed through the hospital's doors feared going blind, they decided to change the hospital's demeanor and service to try and ease those anxieties. "For many people, a visit to the hospital is accompanied by a certain degree of uncertainty and anxiety. There's a good reason that anxiety reduction is an important theme for hospitals," said Dr. Dirk Deichmann, who conducted Design Thinking research with the hospital.

They began brainstorming ideas with members of their staff, with peers in the eye medicine field, and with other businesses in the Netherlands that had a reputation for strong customer service like KLM, the country's flagship airline. They tested those ideas through a series of small experiments with patients of all ages to see which methods would actually reduce the amount of fear people felt while in the hospital. Most of the experiments were informal and inexpensive; they focused more on small and powerful changes instead of expensive purchases.

As should be expected, while some of these ideas worked, others failed. Successful experiments included the practice of sending children who were scheduled to stay in the hospital

T-shirts with animals on them prior to their stay. When the children arrived at the hospital, they were greeted by doctors who wore pins of the same animal, immediately giving the children a topic of conversation and a connection to their care providers and significantly reducing their fear levels.

Another successful initiative was the launch of a mobile app that let patients follow a checklist of all aspects of their care and how things were progressing. This gave patients a clear view of their treatment plans and helped them understand how far they had to go before they would be able to leave the hospital.

Over time, the experiments that were successful were broadly implemented throughout the hospital. The unsuccessful efforts were explored from other angles, but were set aside if they weren't helpful to patients.

What was the impact? Rotterdam Eye patients now heal more quickly, employees are happier in the workplace, patient intake rose by 47 percent over the course of ten years, and the hospital receives high marks in customer service and medical care from its patients.

"Instead of coming up with your own thoughts about what is best for the customer, Design Thinking gives you real insight into what they want," shared Dr. Deichmann.

DREAM BIG, BE PERSISTENT, AND MAKE A DIFFERENCE

As you dive into Design Thinking and creating a new solution, be patient with yourself and with your team. Your first idea (or your first few!) may fall flat. That's all a part of the process. Trust yourselves to learn more about the problem, the stakeholders, and the nuances of a potential solution as you forge on.

"Design Thinking is a series of small steps," emphasizes Professor Lenzi. "It's done in a loop. You prototype the idea, you test it with a small handful of customers and users. You get feedback, and then you tweak it. You do another loop, and you do another loop. That loop process is intended to refine and mature the idea."

You may find that your group's ideas don't revolve around technology. That's absolutely fine. Sometimes, technology *isn't* the best answer. What matters is that you and your team come together to try and make the world a better place.

(SOME OF) THE TOOLS OF INNOVATION

Now that you're familiar with how other people are using technology to make a difference, it's a great time to learn more about the different tools that are available to you for your own efforts. If you're already well-versed in these tech tools, feel free to jump ahead, but it may be worthwhile to get a refresher.

ARTIFICIAL INTELLIGENCE (AI)

WHAT IS ARTIFICIAL INTELLIGENCE?

Artificial intelligence is a tool we can use to "teach" technology how to complete tasks or achieve goals. Using programming codes, the languages we use to talk to computers, we can ask technology to make decisions or complete tasks based on the information we share with it. One example of artificial intelligence in action are wildlife cameras that we use to capture photos of species in their home habitats. The cameras are programmed to wake up and take pictures any time they "see" movement. Then, the photos are shared with an artificial intelligence program that can identify the species photographed. This AI is beneficial because it can review, tag, and catalogue thousands of pictures, which would take a lot of time for a human to do by hand. The AI can then share a report on what animals passed by the camera with researchers around the world. In their design and functionality, technologies that use artificial intelligence copy human thought processes like learning and problem-solving. They are most often used for logistics, data mining, medical diagnosis, and scientific research.

HOW DOES IT WORK?

AI is usually designed to achieve a goal or complete a task using rules to guide decision-making. However, many assigned goals are complex and can be challenging to solve. This is where machine learning comes in. AI is often programmed to learn through time and repetition, which allows it to understand when it has succeeded or failed the task. As the AI learns new ways to succeed, it can spot patterns and change its decision-making to increase its chances of success. To use a human example, if you ate pomegranate ten times and you became sick ten times, you would likely conclude that you may be allergic to pomegranate. AI learns in a similar way and uses that understanding to analyze data and solve problems that would have previously required human intervention.

HAVE I EVER HEARD OF A SUCCESSFUL AI EFFORT?

Famous examples of AI include Deep Blue, the chess-playing computer system that defeated a reigning world champion, and IBM's Watson, which won *Jeopardy!* against two prior champions during a special episode of the iconic TV gameshow.

An example you may be more familiar with is Apple's personal assistant program Siri, which uses voice recognition and artificial intelligence to answer questions, make recommendations, and perform actions based on voice commands. Over time, as an Apple user relies on Siri, the program learns more about its user and adapts to meet their preferences and needs. This kind of learning has a lot of potential for scientific research, conversation, sustainability, development, health, and more.

THIS SOUNDS TOO GOOD TO BE TRUE.

That's because—for now—it is. While artificial intelligence has promise, it has just as many shortcomings. For one, AI lacks what we would consider common sense reasoning, things that we as humans have never been taught but innately understand.

"The great irony of common sense—and indeed AI itself—is that it is stuff that pretty much everybody knows, yet nobody seems to know what exactly it is or how to build machines that possess it," says Gary Marcus, CEO and founder of AI company Robust.AI.

As an example, an AI language program may be asked to complete the sentence "Carol puts a new flower on her sunny patio, and…" A human might say "the flower will thrive in the sunshine" or "it will be lovely décor," as those are both likely outcomes. However, in similar exercises, AI has finished the sentence with comically unexpected lines like "the plant is now missing from the other room."

Another issue is that, like humans, AI can come away from a learning experience with the wrong impression of the correct answer. As an example, when reviewing photos of animals of different colors to identify them, AI may notice that many of the cows are white and therefore conclude that any white animal is a cow.

ISN'T THERE SOME CONTROVERSY REGARDING AI?

AI was initially explored in the 1940s by Alan Turing based on the idea that human intelligence could be replicated by machines. As time has gone on and AI has evolved, people have begun to question the ethics of copying the human mind. AI-related debates include the question of slavery ("if we create something to be intelligent simply to benefit from its work, is that not a form of cruelty?"), the potential for future human job losses ("if we have robots to do jobs that are currently done by humans, won't that leave many people out of a job?"), and the possibility of designing our own downfall ("if we create machines that are as intelligent as humans, couldn't we be creating something that will later destroy us?").

SO WHY CONSIDER USING AI?

While it is controversial and still a bit rough around the edges, AI is already changing the way we analyze data and make decisions. They are undistracted, solely focused on whatever mission they have been designed to achieve. Unlike us, they can think around the clock and present us with summarized findings of mountains of data in only a few hours. In our journey to save the world, artificial intelligence is vulnerable, yet invaluable.

HOW ARE WE USING AI TO "SAVE THE WORLD"?

We've begun using AI to help us analyze data and research in fields ranging from sustainability and energy to health. Because AI can work around the clock, we're able to test ideas more quickly and solve problems using more information than we ever have in the past.

AI is also helping amplify human expertise, sometimes in unexpected ways. One recent and surprising example can be found in the bakeries of Japan. Bakeries that sell a wider variety of pastries were found to have higher sales, and over time, they began offering hundreds of types of pastries for sale each day. When humans were needed to identify and ring up the pastries, it took a long time to train new employees and making purchases could take quite a bit of time. To solve this problem, an engineering company named BRAIN created an artificial intelligence program called BakeryScan that could quickly learn the different types of pastries based on their shapes and appearance and ring up the total cost of a customer's order in seconds.

As BakeryScan began to attract attention, a cancer doctor saw a report about the AI program on TV. As he watched the report, it occurred to him that cancer cells sometimes looked like bread shapes. An idea clicked, and he reached out to BRAIN. The engineering team worked to adapt the program to scan cancer cells instead of pastries. Today, BakeryScan's sister Cyto-Aiscan is used to detect cancer cells, a skill that once required a specialist.

DRONES

WHAT ARE DRONES?

Drones are remote controlled aircraft or seacraft that vary widely from one another. Like land vehicles, drones have a range of uses and their designs can be different based on their purpose. Some drones can use global positioning system (GPS) technology to navigate, and many are equipped with sensors, cameras, and robotic components. Even though they've been used around the world for more than twenty years, drones are a relatively new technology outside of military spaces and are only expected to become more popular in the years to come. Some technologists think we will consider them commonplace by 2030.

WHAT'S THE BENEFIT TO USING DRONES?

Because they are usually modest in size and able to fly long distances, they can easily reach locations that are remote or difficult for people to access. Many can carry packages, take photo or video, be controlled with something as simple as a smartphone app, and many have long-range flight times. While some drones designed for specific purposes can be expensive, basic drones including flight, remote control functionality, and photo/video cameras are relatively affordable and can cost less than five hundred dollars.

WHAT ARE THEIR WEAKNESSES?

Drones are far from a perfect science. As previously mentioned, custom built drones can be prohibitively expensive. They also pose a hazard to aerospace safety because they can interfere with planes and helicopters. Their small size makes them difficult to spot and avoid while in flight, and if they collide with another aircraft, it can lead to catastrophic accidents. Like other aircraft, they can also fail in flight, resulting in crashes that could harm people or animals on the ground. In one example, fifteen hundred bird eggs were abandoned by their parents when a hobbyist accidentally crashed a drone at a nature reserve in Southern California. The three thousand birds that fled, scared by the crash, didn't return to their nests in time to incubate the eggs.

To try and address these issues, many governments have begun to limit how and where drones can be used. Small, flying cameras also come with obvious privacy concerns. Drones can fly nearly anywhere, even over private property. Finally, like any other technology, they do require a certain level of training for proper use and ongoing maintenance.

HOW ARE WE USING DRONES TO "SAVE THE WORLD"?

Drones have a wide range of uses depending on how they are designed. They can be used for surveillance, environment scanning, photography, real estate and construction planning, deliveries, disaster relief, agriculture, search and rescue, warfare, wildlife identification and tracking, and more. We're already using drones to monitor illegal rainforest logging and burning, plant trees in areas ravaged by wild fires, and search rubble for survivors of natural or manmade disasters. We've also begun using drones for business purposes. Companies including Amazon, UPS, and even Domino's have begun to use drones to deliver packages and pizzas to our homes.

SOCIAL MEDIA

WE'VE ALL HEARD THE TERM "SOCIAL MEDIA," BUT WHAT DOES IT MEAN?

Social media is hard to define because of the wide range of platforms it includes. In general, however, social media encourages social interaction and engagement through user-generated content like pictures, videos, stories, and other forms of media. As anyone with an Instagram account knows, the voices of many crowd and compete with one another to grab attention, raise awareness for a cause, or amplify calls for action.

WHAT ARE SOME SOCIAL MEDIA PLATFORMS?

Some of the largest and best-known social media applications include:

- Facebook
- YouTube
- Twitter
- Instagram
- TikTok
- Snapchat
- WhatsApp
- Reddit
- LinkedIn
- Pinterest

New platforms pop up all the time while others fade to the background, and the popularity of these platforms seems to change overnight. Different platforms also appeal to different groups of people. Facebook is a popular social media tool for older generations while TikTok and Instagram are favorites of teenagers.

HOW CAN WE USE SOCIAL MEDIA TO "SAVE THE WORLD"?

While many people use social media to raise awareness around their work or for sales/fundraising, I find it can be most powerful when used to connect with other people who share similar interests and passions. It can be a great tool to find other people who want to solve some of the world's biggest challenges and may be interested in collaborating with you. As you begin sharing information about your innovation efforts or projects, focus on *connecting* with others rather than *broadcasting* your progress. Participate in Twitter chats using hashtags, share kudos with your teammates on LinkedIn, and participate in Facebook group discussions about climate change or animal conservation. Focus on having conversations with people interested in or working on similar efforts. Building a network of collaborators through social media has many best practices. Although we won't cover them in this book, I recommend doing some quick googling to explore them and find what works best for you.

ISN'T SOCIAL MEDIA CONTROVERSIAL?

Increasingly so. Social media has become a primary source for misinformation, ranging from flat Earth conspiracies to anti-vaccination theories to cult-like political circles. As an example, *Scientific American* found that the rise of conspiracy theories over social media was identified as one of the key contributors to the 2021 Capitol Riot attack in Washington,

DC. Misinformation spreads so quickly because social media relies upon user-generated conversations and content to thrive. This makes platforms hesitant to censor or monitor users, even those who spread false information.

SO WHAT CAN I DO?

If you do take to social media to build your network or share your innovation story, try to share information that is up-to-date and accurate. If you make a mistake, be willing to address and correct it. Engage and interact with other trustworthy people or groups. Try not to be pulled into circular debates or online squabbles, as many are started by people looking to spread false information through public disagreements. Remember *why* you are turning to social media as a tool—to spread the word about work that you hope will build a better world.

MOBILE TECHNOLOGIES

WHAT DO YOU MEAN BY MOBILE TECHNOLOGIES?

In the most common of terms, cell phones! But a mobile technology includes any portable computing device that helps us communicate with one another. Other examples include smartwatches and tablets, such as iPads.

CELL PHONES ARE COMMON KNOWLEDGE. WHY ARE THEY IMPORTANT?

Smartphones and cell phones are pervasive technologies. According to the Pew Research Center, "it is estimated that more than five billion people have mobile devices, and over half of these connections are smartphones." *Time* magazine reports that more people have access to cell phones than to toilets. In many countries, citizens do not have any access to a computer or to the Internet other than by using their cell phone.

WHAT ARE THE DOWNSIDES OF MOBILE TECHNOLOGY?

The most prevalent downside in 2021 is privacy. Technology companies—including Google, Apple, and Facebook—have been quietly collecting data points on mobile users. Lengthy mobile app Terms & Conditions have led billions of people around the world to let companies track every tap, text, purchase and, in some cases, conversations. These data points are used to track trends in different demographics, to sell targeted products to mobile phone users, and are sometimes even sold to third parties.

HOW CAN WE USE MOBILE TECHNOLOGIES TO "SAVE THE WORLD"?

When thinking of innovative solutions to bring to low-income countries where resources like electricity and Internet aren't as plentiful, creating solutions that are accessible by cell phone may be one of the best ways to connect with local stakeholders. Creating new initiatives that connect to mobile technologies can also give you access to a large, worldwide audience.

5G

I'VE HEARD A LOT ABOUT 5G, 4G, 3G...WHAT ARE THEY?

5G, 4G, and 3G are all forms of cellular wireless technology. They transmit data, like the Internet and your favorite cat memes, to and from mobile devices. The different "Gs" detail how the networks connect to the Internet using radio waves at varying frequencies. In 2021, 5G has been a hot topic due to both its pending worldwide rollout and online misinformation about its purpose and function.

SPEAKING OF, HOW DO I SURVIVE THE PENDING 5G APOCALYPSE?

Just kidding, of course. While there's a lot of bad information floating around about 5G, it's not at all dangerous to humans or to animals. It doesn't cause cancer, it doesn't kill birds, it doesn't lead to autism, and it wasn't sneakily injected into people who got the COVID-19 vaccines. It's just a network that can get you your cat memes faster than ever before.

HOW CAN WE USE 5G TO "SAVE THE WORLD"?

As of the initial writing of this book (published in 2021), it's difficult to say. There are a lot of big promises from mobile technology vendors about what 5G will mean for the world and for innovation, but it is still not widely available at time of this publication. That being said, 5G will make it easier and faster to generate, share, and collect large amounts of data. That data won't just be to and from our computers to our smartphones; it will also likely increase the reliability of and our reliance on sensors and the Internet of Things.

INTERNET OF THINGS (IOT)

THE INTERNET OF WHAT NOW?

Now we're getting into the sci-fi stuff! With the rise of technologies and our increasing reliance upon the conveniences it brings, we've begun to see a convergence (or a merging) of technology with other tools and appliances that we frequently use. Using sensors and cellular broadband technologies (like 5G), we're able to gather large amounts of data and react to that data even when we're not physically present. As an example, people who manage building maintenance can use IoT sensors to monitor and control building temperatures, lock or unlock doors, measure energy use, measure water use, and more. A building's sensors can even be set up to note when more people are in a room than usual and use historical data of temperature increases to preemptively lower the temperature to make the room more comfortable.

HOW COMMON IS IOT?

A common use of Internet of Things in 2021 are smart home devices, like smart thermometers that connect to our smartphones and doorbells that begin video recording any time they detect movement at our front doors. Amazon's Alexa and other digital home assistants are other common examples of Internet of Things devices. We've also begun to see IoT techniques applied to cars (remote start and lock, etc.) and other devices like refrigerators, baby monitors, and security cameras. IoT is also increasingly utilized in business settings, everywhere from manufacturing plants (to monitor operational systems effectiveness and health) to high-rise offices (to manage temperature, monitor resource availability, and control lighting and other electrical commands from afar). As 5G is rolled out and cellular broadband can handle larger amounts of data more quickly, we'll see a continued rise in IoT technologies.

AS WITH EVERY OTHER TECHNOLOGY WE'VE TALKED ABOUT, WHAT'S THE CATCH?

Privacy and security. The more these sensors are integrated into our day-to-day lives, the more the companies that manage the collected data will come to learn about us. That information can be sold, used to advertise or sell to us, or used to monitor our decision-making to inform the development of future products and services (so, selling to us with extra steps). We also often have little insight into where our data is going or how it's being stored. Someone may not be too concerned with their smart thermostat knowing that they like to keep their home at a toasty seventy-three degrees, but they likely wouldn't want their digital baby monitor storing video of their young child in a corporate cloud server.

HOW CAN WE USE IOT TO "SAVE THE WORLD"?

Possibilities for small IoT sensors that can detect things like temperature, movement, humidity, and more are almost limitless. IoT is best used in scenarios where ongoing monitoring of an area would help solve the problem. Because the sensors keep working twenty-four hours a day and don't need to rest or take a lunch break, they can keep collecting and sharing data.

One example of using IoT to make a difference can be found in South Africa, where a team of experts was working to defend a game reserve's endangered rhinos from poachers. The experts found that IoT sensors could be placed on animals of different species in the reserve to track their motion and see if something had startled them or caused them to flee, like a potential poacher. They put special collars on hundreds of their animals of all species to track their movement and the animals' reactions to being startled would alert the experts that the reserve's rhinos were in danger.

ROBOTS

EVERYONE KNOWS WHAT A ROBOT IS.

In general, yes. Most people know that robots are machines that can be designed to complete a task or to take a specific action. Robots have become increasingly common in manufacturing, mining, farming, and other industries. We usually hear about robots as they relate to automation and changes in labor markets. As robotics becomes a more sophisticated field, and as AI continues to mature, robots will be able to take on more tasks that are done by humans today. While that is a point of concern for policymakers and economists, it can be of benefit to innovators.

HOW CAN WE USE ROBOTS TO "SAVE THE WORLD"?

However we design them! Some robots are designed and built to function autonomously, to run a program over and over again until it is given a different directive. Others are built to be operated from afar, essentially extending the reach of potential human intervention into the previously mentioned difficult-to-withstand spaces. If programmed correctly and built with the right materials, robots can work in conditions that are inhospitable to humans. They can work in the bitter cold or in the severe heat. They can work in low- or no-oxygen environments, including space and the surfaces of other planets. As machines, they do not need to sleep or rest. They can be programmed to operate continuously for a set amount of time to complete a task. Robots are also fantastic candidates for jobs that are tedious, repetition based, or straight up boring.

DATA, BIG DATA, AND DATA ANALYTICS

WHAT IS DATA?

The Merriam-Webster Dictionary defines data as "factual information (such as measurements or statistics) used as a basis for reasoning, discussion, or calculation" and "information in digital form that can be transmitted or processed." In layman terms, data are points of information that can be collected and used to draw conclusions or help inform decision-making.

THAT'S PRETTY VAGUE.

Unfortunately, yes! Data can be almost any type of information you can imagine. The temperature of your home city at 2:00 p.m. this coming Friday is a data point. Your personal email address is a data point. The price of your Netflix subscription (two dollars more per month by the time this book is published) is a data point. By themselves, these pieces of information are only so valuable. By drawing them together and analyzing them against other pieces of data, we can use that information to draw conclusions or find new questions.

OKAY, BUT WHAT ABOUT "BIG DATA"?

As technology has continued to progress, so too has our ability to store information and—you guessed it—data. Just like your iPhone or computer, the world has a maximum storage capacity, and it has been increasing year over year since the 1980s. As our collective capacity has grown, the amount of data we could collect and store has grown as well. Meanwhile, our day-to-day reliance on devices that generate data like mobile phones, computers, and software has continued to grow. As data is generated, it is often gathered and saved to be used for later analysis. This has given rise to "big data," or the use of large data sets of aggregate and related data that can be used to visualize trends, conduct research, and even predict human and market behaviors.

In one real example of this scenario, a father learned that his teenage daughter was pregnant when she received a flyer from Target congratulating her and inviting her to open a registry with the chain. Target's marketing department had identified what types of products newly pregnant women purchased and were able to track the woman's purchases with their store through their loyalty program. The chain's data was so detailed that they were able to track how far along a woman's pregnancy had progressed, sometimes before the women themselves even knew they were pregnant.

SO DATA ANALYTICS IS...

The analysis of data sets (or big data) to inform decision-making or courses of action in government, scientific research, business, healthcare, finance...you name it. Data analytics are often designed to be interactive using dashboards that can explore specific questions or elements of a topic.

HOW CAN WE USE ALL OF THIS TO "SAVE THE WORLD"?

Data can help us identify trends, spot correlations, and make new discoveries about the world. In one example, a team of scientists collaborating with NOAA used big data collected about whale feeding grounds to help create a tool that prevents ships from running into endangered whales. The whale detection system, Whale Safe, uses big data modeling to predict the likelihood of a whale being in a ship's vicinity. This information is then shared with ships, which are able to slow down to prevent colliding with and fatally injuring a whale.

PROGRAMMING, CODING, DEVELOPING, AND LANGUAGES

THERE'S A LOT GOING ON IN THAT HEADING.

True, and if I were writing a book about computer programming, I wouldn't toss all of those topics into one section. But for our purposes, I think tackling all of these in one spot will help you see how they all tie together.

OKAY. SO, WHAT IS PROGRAMMING?

Computer programming is the act of writing a program that tells a computer how we want it to complete a task. As an example, when you click on the X button at the top of your Internet browser, the programming is what tells your browser that it should close. Programming is also referred to as developing or coding. Similarly, people who program are known as programmers, developers, or coders.

WHAT DO YOU MEAN BY LANGUAGES?

Developers use "languages" to talk to the computer or software to tell it what to do, how, and in what order. Those languages can include:

- Python
- JavaScript
- Java
- C++
- HTML
- CSS

WHY ARE THERE SO MANY LANGUAGES?

The languages serve different roles. JavaScript is one of the most popular languages for building websites because it allows for significant interactivity. Python is a heavy hitter in the data analysis and artificial intelligence fields. CSS and HTML are both used to design the look and feel of websites.

AND DEVELOPERS KNOW ALL OF THESE LANGUAGES?

No! Even developers typically have very specific skill sets. A web developer would frequently use HTML and CSS to design, create, and maintain websites, but they likely wouldn't know how to use Python for data analysis. When bringing a team together to tackle one of our world's big challenges, remember that there is no "one size fits all developer." While it will be great to have someone with technical experience on your team, don't expect them to know every language. They may need to reach out to their network to find someone with the expertise you need down the line.

HOW CAN WE USE PROGRAMMING TO "SAVE THE WORLD"?

Many idealistic innovation technology projects are going to use some form of programming. Whether it's creating a new phone app to help citizen scientists share whale sightings to a virtual reality game that lets the viewer step into the history of the Underground Railroad, programming will be the bones of your project. Even if you use user-friendly tools that do all the programming for you like "what you see is what you get" website or mobile app builders, there will still be programming going on in the background. If you're not a programming type of person, don't worry. People who know how to code and would love to put their talents to use to make the world a better place are countless.

NOTHING IS PERMANENT BUT CHANGE

Tech to Save the World was written and published in 2021. Depending on when you're reading this, a lot may have changed over the years! Technology advances quickly, gaining more speed every day. If you'd like to read more about the latest and greatest since the early 2020s, I recommend doing some quick googling around "emerging technologies."

THE BLUEPRINTS TO BUILDING A BETTER WORLD

11

BLUEPRINT: FOR DREAMERS

BLUEPRINT FOR DREAMERS

Dreamers are the readers who have limited access to resources (money, team members, support) but who still want to start making a difference in the world. Examples of dreamers include students, entrepreneurs, new nonprofit founders, and professionals who work in spaces that do not align with their world-changing goals. While the characters and stories highlighted in this section are fictitious, they are inspired by real-life idealistic innovation projects.

MEET MATT

Matt was a rising Senior studying Government Relations at an American university. Matt studied government because he was passionate about climate change and species conservation, and he hoped to make the world a better place by working at a government agency or for a nonprofit.

Unfortunately, Matt had been feeling a bit disillusioned. During his two internships, he didn't really feel connected to the work. As an intern, he spent most of his time at a desk checking emails and writing memos. Matt wished he could do something immediately to help the environment or make a difference in climate change.

One day, Matt came across an article about how 40 percent of American honeybees had died in one year. The article explained that bees were dying at an alarming rate due to habitat loss and increased use of pesticides. Frustrated, Matt shared the article with his girlfriend. "Can you believe this?" he asked. "Why aren't they doing anything about this?"

After a few minutes, she replied. "I saw...Poor bees! They who, though? Whose job is it to try and save the bees? Wish we could do something."

*Matt paused, thinking about her reply. Really, who **were** the people who were supposed to be saving the bees? Government employees? Nonprofits? Farmers?*

Maybe it was supposed to be people like him. "Maybe we can. Let's meet at the library; I have an idea." Matt grabbed his laptop and a few textbooks and dashed out the door. It was time to start saving the bees. But where to start?

1) FIRST, FIND THE PROBLEM OR CHALLENGE YOU WANT TO SOLVE FOR.

Before we can find solutions to problems, we need to understand the root causes of the problems instead of focusing on the symptoms.

When you have a passion for something, it can be frustrating to sit around thinking about the problem rather than working to solve it. Still, a little bit of forethought and preplanning can go a long way and can make whatever solution you create more impactful. To get started, find a specific challenge to address rather than a broad one; **narrow your focus to increase your impact.**

To find the problem or challenge you want to solve for, try any of the following:

- Researching root causes of the issue
- Doing the Five Whys exercise (covered in Chapter 9 "Design Thinking—Dreaming to Big Ideas")
- Interviewing subject matter experts, researchers, and others with significant experience with the problem

Matt and his girlfriend met at the library and, using the article as a starting point, began to research why bees were dying off so quickly. They discovered that a world-renowned ento-mologist (a person who studies bugs), Dr. Collins, worked at their university. They sent an email to her office asking to meet with her and she invited them to come by the next day.

Dr. Collins was passionate about saving the bees too, and she happily shared a lot of insights that were more detailed than any of the articles they had read. She told them one of the primary reasons for bee die-off was loss of habitat due to increased need for farming land.

Leaving the interview, Matt decided he wanted to do some-thing to help create more space for bees to live across the country. But he knew he wouldn't be able to do it alone.

2) FIND LIKEMINDED PEOPLE WHO HAVE A SIMILAR INTEREST

While you *can* build a better world on your own, blazing a trail with a team is more likely to lead to success and greater impact (see Chapter 4 "Collaborating"). Having a team can result in more ideas for solutions, help catch mistakes before they become catastrophic, and provide access to a wider range of skills that can help address the challenge. **When you have an idea of a big challenge that you want to take on, start by finding your team.**

If you're also the type of person who wants to put your skills to use but don't know what issue you want to address, you can use these same methods to find a team to join and support.

Ideas for finding your team include:

- Social media
- School/professional networks
- Hackathons
- Professional organizations (some offer discounted student memberships)

Once you've connected with others who share your interest, you can encourage them to collaborate with you by appealing to their passion for the cause, their expertise in the field, or your willingness to put in the effort needed to make the project successful.

After meeting with Dr. Collins, Matt made a brief presentation on the problems facing the bees and shared it during one of his business fraternity meetings. He asked if anyone would like to work on the project, and he also requested that the group connect him with anyone they knew of who may be interested in the topic.

In the end, Matt's team grew from two (Matt and his girlfriend, Sadie) to six; two business fraternity members asked how they could help out, one student connected Matt with her roommate who had experience with beekeeping, and another was connected to the team through social media after a fraternity member tweeted about the presentation.

Matt set up a group chat, and everyone agreed to connect after classes the next week to get started.

3) POOL YOUR SKILLS

With your team assembled, get everyone together for introductions and share how you developed an interest in the problem. Have everyone discuss their educational and/or professional backgrounds. Then, give everyone in the room a stack of Post-it Notes (ideally different colors for different people) and a pen. Take five minutes to have everyone list out as many skills that they have (or would like to develop) on individual sticky notes, building a pile in front of them.

Encourage team members to dig deep. What are computer programs they used for school projects? Do they have any artistic hobbies? Anything and everything is relevant here in the ideation phase.

Afterward, have each person talk through all of their sticky notes and place them on a wall or white board. Group similar skills (for example, data, data science, Python, analytics) together in categories. When you're done, take a step back and talk through the skills and experiences you bring as a group.

Based on the skills you've laid out, define some tentative roles for the team. If someone is strong in social media and writing, perhaps they can serve as your expertise engagement lead, finding subject matter experts to connect with for interviews and expert guidance. If another team member is comfortable with data analytics, perhaps they can be in charge of finding relevant data sets and sources that can be used for designing or testing the impact of your proposed solution. While assigning roles, keep an open mind to the types of work people are interested in doing. Genuine interest in the topic and their role in the project will encourage people to continue collaborating.

The group of people who wanted to save the bees hadn't previously worked together. Instead of a traditional ice breaker, Matt and the team ran through an exercise to explore what skills and experiences each brought to the team.

- *Matt had a lot of project management experience to help keep the team on track, but he also had some experience in government and nonprofit work through his internships. He also had access to a broader network of start-ups and small companies through his business fraternity.*
- *Sadie brought a background in computer coding; she used Python and other languages for her class projects and shared that she'd like to somehow apply that experience to the solution.*
- *Jenny grew up in a rural community and had a little bit of experience with beekeeping; she would be able to bring the perspective of beekeepers, and also had insights into colony behavior and tools of the trade. She could also help the group connect with current beekeepers.*
- *Devon was studying public relations and frequently used graphic design software for his classes. He was interested in using his communications and design acumen to spread the word about the team's efforts and help with any branding or materials that would be needed.*
- *Claude was studying mathematics and had a specific interest in statistics and research methodology. He*

offered to help conduct background research on the program, dig up relevant statistics that might help the team better understand the nuances of the problem, and lead the development and analysis of any surveys or firsthand research the group may need to conduct.

- *Initially, Joe was worried her experiences and classes for her education degree wouldn't be very useful to the team. But through discussion, it became clear there would likely be a training or change component to whatever solution they explored. Joe also shared that her father was a carpenter and she knew how to do some woodworking. She volunteered to help if anything needed to be physically built.*

4) BRAINSTORM AS A TEAM

Once you have a team assembled, it's time to brainstorm! Talk through the problem as a group and brainstorm solutions. Remember, this is a time to be creative and outlandish. Don't limit the team just yet—have a "blue sky" conversation where you imagine they have all the skills and resources you need, and anything is possible. This will prevent you from cutting out ideas with potential too early in the brainstorming process. At this point in the process, it's okay to get a little crazy!

If you need some ideas of how to brainstorm, refer back to Chapter 9 "Design Thinking—Dreaming to Big Ideas." A few exercises described there can help you shake the rust off and get creative.

While you're brainstorming, encourage the team to build upon the ideas of others rather than nix ideas early on; advocate for team members using the "yes and" approach, where they build upon one another's perspectives and ideas. Approach challenges from a perspective of "how might we…" rather than "if only…"

Once again, put all your ideas down on paper and start to bucket them. Do you have a lot of great ideas around one element of the root problem? Or does your team find itself gravitating toward a particular solution type? Look at the themes you've proposed and explored through the conversation and make note of those.

You don't need to decide which solution to pursue during that first brainstorming session. Instead, the team should come away with ideas for further research and exploration. Divvy up topics to team members with related interests and start digging.

After getting to know each other, the team began brainstorming—and they had some wild ideas!

- *"What if every farm was federally required to have some bee colonies?"*
- *"What if we created little robots that could identify where bees were losing territory and transform into portable hives for them?"*
- *"What if we created a pesticide that kills everything **but** bees?"*
- *"What if beekeeping had fewer barriers to entry?"*

5) DO SOME RESEARCH TO NARROW DOWN THE OPTIONS

Split up as a team and start doing some research around the ideas you brainstormed. Have similar efforts been done before? If so, where have they failed or succeeded? What opportunities for improvement exist? If it's never been done, is that because it doesn't truly solve the challenge? Or is it just a new angle that hasn't been previously considered?

Even if you find that someone *has* done work similar to what you're considering, that shouldn't deter you. If you and your team have a passion for the effort and have the right skill sets, there may be an opportunity for you to do something similar (or better). Just because it's been done doesn't mean it's been done (or applied) well!

At the same time, you wouldn't start a new phone company and launch straight into challenging Apple or Nokia. If you find that one of your ideas has already been done by an organization that is well-established around the world and can demonstrate significant impact, consider exploring other options.

As you're researching, explore what tools and capabilities you may need to follow through on your idea. Do you need a particular type of hardware or building tool? Can your team afford to purchase one, or can you find one to borrow for free? Do you need a specific skill set or type of expertise to be successful that isn't currently represented on your team?

Research can look like a lot of things. Don't limit yourself to googling (what we in the technology business refer to as "open-source research"). Be willing to explore information you can find in libraries, in scientific journals, or through direct interviews with experts, policymakers, or academics to curate a well-rounded view of the challenge and the solution you're looking to create.

Once you've done your research, come back together as a team to narrow down the options of your initial brainstorm based on what you've learned. Some ideas will get immediately thrown out—they've been done and failed, they're too expensive, they'll require too much specialized equipment. But others will float to the top. Your team has the skills needed, the passion to drive them, and access to the resources that will be needed to create them.

As you're narrowing down your list, think through the following:

- Likely Impact: Will this idea or solution solve for the root of the problem? What will be the range of the potential impact? Will it help a little bit or a lot?
- Ability to Measure: How can you define success with this idea? Will you be able to measure its success quantifiably,

or will it have a less concrete impact? Note that this shouldn't be a disqualifier—many things worth doing aren't yet measurable by hard data—but should be a consideration!

- Tools Needed: Do you have access to everything you'd need to create a prototype or minimum viable product of this idea?
- Time Needed: How long will it take you and your team to create, design, build, and potentially implement this idea? Can the issue at hand wait that long for a solution?
- Resources Needed: How much money will be needed to design, build, and test this? Does your team have access to those types of funds? If not, are there ways that you can request funding (grants, university hackathon contests, etc.)?

Using these criteria as a guide and your team's interests at heart (especially if they're supporting this for free), narrow down your options. Select *one* idea to pursue immediately, but make a note of three to five runner-up ideas to explore if the first option doesn't pan out. When narrowing in on your solution, remember that **you can go big—for a Moonshot—or you can go small—for a single step—but whatever you choose, go forward.**

Armed with this information, the group began to talk through new ways to address the challenge of habitat loss. "Maybe an app?" Sadie proposed. "Tinder for bees? People can go on and offer space on their property to host bees, and people who want to keep bees can agree to care for those bees?"

"Bees for Businesses," quipped Jenny. "Businesses could sponsor a hive and then have first access to that honey to use in their products or even their coffee break rooms or something?"

"Those are good ideas," said Dr. Collins, "but I'm trying to figure out if there's a way we can help bridge this gap between interest and action. Something to make it easy for people to support bees directly and stay engaged."

"You know," said Claude, "my mom just set up a bat house in her backyard. Apparently bats struggle to find places to rest or sleep sometimes, and she said she likes them because they eat the bugs. What if we had bee houses? Like people have bat houses or bird feeders?"

"Those do exist," shared Dr. Collins. "But they can be really dangerous if not done right. It's important to use the right materials and keep it clean—otherwise they can wind up causing more harm than good."

"Maybe we can work together to create a good one," suggested Joe.

6) BE WILLING TO LEARN SOMETHING NEW

When you've narrowed down your potential solutions, you
may find that you are not familiar with all of the tools that
will be needed to begin developing one of the ideas you came
up with. Even if it's not explicitly aligned to your role on
the team, I recommend exploring online courses or other
materials to become more comfortable with the concepts and
content that will be used to bring your idea to life.

*"What kinds of bees do you want to build the houses for?"
asked Dr. Collins.*

"What do you mean?" Sadie replied.

*"Well, people usually think of bees as honeybees, but there
are other types of bees. In fact, honeybees aren't native to
North America. They were brought over by Europeans.
Native bees are usually solitary bees, which don't live in big
hives," shared Dr. Collins. "So the types of wood and the
structure of the homes will be very different based on the
type of bee you pick."*

*"Huh...I'll spend some time reading up on types of bees and
their habitats. Maybe that will help us narrow it down,"
said Matt.*

7) START WORKING—AND GET TO
MINIMUM FUNCTIONALITY

With an idea selected and your team roles identified, it's time to get to work! Work with your team to start building a solution that meets the primary goal of your innovation, even if it lacks all of the bells and whistles that your "ideal" solution might include.

As you're building, bring stakeholders and potential users into the fold early on. If you get their ideas and insights during the development and build phase of your efforts, they'll be able to share perspectives that can help shape your final solution, making it more effective in the long run. As you're working, focus on getting feedback every step of the way. Do potential users of the solution find it effective? Is it helpful? Does it actually address the problem or is it a short-term Band-Aid?

Remember, the focus at this point in time should be creating something that addresses the need but isn't fancy or fully fleshed out. In the technology world, this is known as the "minimum viable product." It's not the end state for your idea. Instead, it will let you test your idea against the problem to see if it is actually making an impact and give you more room to iterate and make improvements moving forward.

The team sketched out a version of what their bee house could be. Along the way, they researched different types of bees and habitats that catered to them. They decided to focus on solitary bees, which are less well-known than traditional honeybees but are more efficient pollinators. They created a small structure that could be placed on the ground or hung from a tree and collaborated with Dr. Collins and Jenny to identify materials that would be safe to use and could be affordable to source. Working together, and with Joe's guidance in the woodshop, they built their first prototype.

Devon took a photo and shared the team's story on Twitter. "Saving our planet, one bee at a time!" The responses were... less than enthusiastic.

- *I don't know...this is a lovely little house, but if it's not kept clean it could possibly kill any bees that live there... People would have to do something to keep it clean.*
- *Wait, why would anyone want to keep a swarm of bees out back? And they don't even get **honey**?*
- *Seems like a nuisance to me. My backyard is already full of pests. Why would I want to add more?*

As the feedback poured in, the team discussed it thoroughly. Even though some of it was harsh, it was valid. More importantly, the constructive criticism helped the team realize they weren't quite sure who their target audience for the bee houses was. Who would have the most use for something like this? And how could it be tweaked to help them have a better understanding of the plight of bees?

8) ITERATE

With your initial prototype ready to go, it's time to iterate! By this point, you've likely shared what you've created so far with users and stakeholders. I also recommend reaching out to share your progress with any experts or academics you connected with to get their perspective and feedback on what you've built so far.

If your solution is some kind of prototype or physical solution, now is the time to give it a test run. Try using it to see how it helps address the problem you're solving for, if at all. Remember to try and use hard data to measure your impact.

After feedback and initial tests, you'll likely note that your MVP isn't performing in quite the way you'd hoped. This is normal and expected!

Take a look at all of the information you gathered. Collaborate with the team to prioritize it. What pieces of feedback were the most impactful in terms of its *effectiveness at addressing the problem?* With prioritization in hand, begin to identify these critical gaps first and work with the team to figure out how to improve your solution to address them, or how to mitigate their impact.

As you're working your way down your list of future iterations, focus your resources and energy on critical needs rather than "nice to haves." If a user has shared feedback that they won't use your solution unless X, explore incorporating X! But if another user says your solution works okay but they'd prefer Y, consider incorporating Y at another time or as resources permit.

While you're refining your solution, encourage the team to get creative with iteration. New feedback and identified shortcomings may require you to go into new rounds of brainstorming of how to incorporate needed features. Don't prioritize the easiest fixes; remember that your initial solution was specifically designed to give you room for future enhancements!

From here, **keep iterating.** You may find your team going into four or five iteration cycles to improve the solution. If you keep your focus on the problem and incorporate relevant feedback from stakeholders, you'll draw closer to a strong solution with each cycle.

"You know," mentioned Sadie, "I was just thinking the other day I could use a Raspberry Pi computer to set up a little counter thing on the house, that would just count how many bees fly in and out of the house. So you could see that there were twenty bees in residence or something, and watch that number grow over time."

"That's awesome," said Devon. "We could even set it up to auto-Tweet, you know, like some companies do? 'twelve bees abuzzin' today!'"

"Could we also find a way to monitor that the bee house is getting too dirty and needs to be cleaned?" asked Jenny.

"Hmm," Sadie murmured. "I can look into those ideas! They're a bit more complicated, but I'll see what I can come up with."

"Sounds like we have a plan," said Matt. "Let's get to work!"

9) KNOW WHEN TO SCRAP

Sometimes all of our ideas and good intentions and resources just don't cut it. If you're continuing to iterate and test your solution and you're not having the impact you were hoping for, don't be afraid to put the project on pause and try something else.

Be willing and open to exploring other avenues or building out your other ideas that were placed on the back burner. Even if your initial prototype is never applied to the final solution, it doesn't mean the effort is wasted. You and your team will have learned what *doesn't* work, which is some of the most powerful learning and information that can be found. You will apply those lessons learned to your final solution and it will be more impactful and meaningful because of them.

10) LAUNCH

So you've built a prototype or solution, you've gathered user feedback, you've iterated on the initial solution, and all of your testing says that what you've built *can* and *does* have an impact on the root problem you've been looking to solve for. Congratulations! You've *already begun* changing the world. Now it's time to amplify that impact.

When your project is ready for prime time, consider partnering with other entities (businesses, nonprofits, NGOs, government grants, etc.) to either request further development funding, tweak and roll out the solution, or bring it to the consumer market. In some cases, you may even want to explore using your solution to begin a start-up and explore outside investor funding.

Begin sharing the story of what you've created on your social media networks, your school networks (including alumni associations), and through personal connections to tell the story of what you've been working on and share your innovation with the world.

Try to identify funding organizations that have a vested interest in the problem you're looking to solve for. Many organizations provide grant funding for new ideas or business opportunities, while others partner directly to try and bring the solutions to those who need them most. Once again, connect with the experts who have provided their insight along the way to ask about the best way to apply your solution to the problem.

In finding resources on how and when best to partner, googling is going to be one of the strongest tools you have. This space changes so quickly, with new resources and opportunities at every turn, that anything published in this book would be out of date by the time it went to print. The best way you can apply your solution to the problem will depend on the type of solution you've created—but by this point, through your iteration and brainstorming and stakeholder engagement, you should have a good idea of what that best avenue will be.

If it doesn't garner interest immediately, don't be let down. As we talked about earlier, this is a time of unprecedented technology change. Some solutions garner attention through international media publications like the *New York Times*, while others are procured directly by nonprofit organizations looking to apply solutions. Even others take the world by storm through informal social media channels like TikTok.

If you have a good idea, and you can prove that it will make an impact on the world, you *can and will* find a way to apply it directly to the problem. It may take time and tenacity, but you've already proven that you care enough about this issue to spend both.

If you find yourself stuck, remember—I'm team member number two. You can always reach me at www.techtosavethe-world.com and I'll do my best to help!

After a few months of work and research, the team was ready to launch the Bee Together program pilot. They had worked together to build sizeable bee houses out of sustainable materials and rig each one up with solar-powered sensors that monitored how many bees were in residence.

They had also collaborated with Dr. Collins, local beekeepers, and educators from Joe's network to create an educational program for primary school students. The program included content on the lives of solitary bees, how they differed from honeybees, the role they played in pollination, and care information to keep the bee houses safe and clean for their new residents.

Matt collaborated with the university's Office of Government Affairs to explore state and federal grants for education programs, and together the team prepared a successful submission. They received a grant for thirty-five thousand dollars to build bee houses and begin piloting their program at schools around the state.

As pilots kicked off, Devon created and shared content of the pilot on social media. Over time, it gained traction, and people began reaching out to the team to ask about how they could bring the program to their local schools. Meanwhile, with some viral marketing on Devon's part, interest in a home version of the bee houses grew as well. Claude developed a survey to learn more about what home consumers would look for in a bee home and analyzed the information to recommend changes for a second prototype to the team. With that information in hand, the team created a new design that would fit in people's backyards. Sadie continued applying her development acumen to dive into a new skill, mobile app development, which she used to build an app that accompanied the home-style bee houses and shared how many bees of what types were in residence at any given time.

12

BLUEPRINT: FOR PROFESSIONALS

BLUEPRINT FOR PROFESSIONALS

Professionals are the readers who currently work in a setting that allows them access to some resources (funding available for special projects, team member availability, job alignment to the goal). Professionals include people who work at nonprofit organizations, technology professionals working at companies that provide time or money for research and development, or people working at organizations that set aside funding for philanthropy or special projects. While the characters and stories highlighted in this section are fictitious, they are inspired by real-life idealistic innovation projects.

Sarah worked as a program manager at Archways, a non-profit that provided health and care services for people with mental disabilities. She found the organization was struggling with keeping staff who could provide services for people in the nonprofit's care; the organization had a limited budget and could only afford to pay so much, and candidates who applied for jobs were often unfamiliar with working with people with mental disabilities. They struggled to support clients who would act out or behave erratically, and many of the staff would either do the exact wrong thing out of lack of understanding or would quit after realizing how challenging the job would be.

Sarah knew there had to be a way to either attract more prepared candidates for job openings or help current staff prepare for challenging situations. She approached her boss, the Archways Director Ben, and asked to spend some time exploring the challenge. He approved of her spending the time to come up with some unique solutions, but warned that the nonprofit didn't have much money available for special projects.

1) FIRST, FIND THE PROBLEM OR CHALLENGE YOU WANT TO SOLVE FOR.

In Chapter 9 "Design Thinking—Dreaming to Big Ideas," we talked about the importance of understanding the root causes of the problem we're working to solve. Before we jump into finding solutions, we need to be sure we're not just focusing on symptoms of the problem. While addressing symptoms can be beneficial, we may not have the impact we are hoping for in the long run.

A little bit of forethought and preplanning can go a long way and can make whatever solution you create more impactful. To get started, find a specific challenge to address rather than a broad one; **narrow your focus to increase your impact.**

Start by:

- Researching root causes of the issue
- Doing the Five Whys exercise (covered in Chapter 9 "Design Thinking—Dreaming to Big Ideas")
- Interviewing subject matter experts, researchers, and others with significant experience with the problem

Sarah and Ben discussed the problem in detail together. Ben shared the organization's financials with Sarah, and together they concluded there was no way they could afford to pay staff (and potentially more qualified, trained candidates) more money. Sarah had initially been hoping to explore a new hiring program that would target graduating college students who had specialized in psychology or counseling, but the funding available wouldn't allow them to offer competitive salaries.

Sarah and Ben shifted their focus and began to explore the other potential avenue—training and readiness of current staff. Walking through a Five Whys exercise, they determined their staff was unprepared for crises or behavioral challenges because of limited experience working with people with mental disabilities. Unfortunately, it seemed their current training methods weren't as impactful as they could be.

2) EXPLORE OPPORTUNITIES TO SOLVE THE PROBLEM WITHIN YOUR PROFESSIONAL SPHERE

As a professional, you may have access to networks and resources that can help you get started when looking to solve for the problem you're passionate about. If you work in a large company or a nonprofit, ask around to see if there are employee interest groups or communities of practice that focus on innovation or corporate social responsibility opportunities. In some cases, large companies and nonprofits set aside funding for employee-led innovation efforts.

If the problem you're looking to solve is somehow related to your day-to-day work, talk to your boss. There may be funding available for business development or corporate innovation efforts which could be used to bring together an internal team to innovate around the challenge.

If such groups do not exist in your workplace, turn your gaze outward. Look into professional associations that may align with your professional background that have subgroups related to your topic of interest. Explore opportunities to participate in hackathons for working professionals or take to social media to connect with other professionals looking to apply their skills toward a problem they're passionate about. This is a great opportunity to draw in expertise from people working in different fields for collaboration!

While Archways wasn't a very large nonprofit, Ben was a member of a network of similar nonprofits across the region. He sent an email out to his network of other executives asking if they had any team members who would be interested in collaborating with Sarah to explore ways to improve their training methods. The response was immediate and enthusiastic; two nonprofit executives replied, each volunteering members of their teams to share their experiences and collaborate on the challenge.

3) POOL YOUR SKILLS

Once you've found a few people to collaborate with, get everyone together for a kickoff session. Introduce yourselves and share a bit about your backgrounds and your experiences with the problem. Then, give everyone in the room a stack of Post-it Notes (different colors for different people!) and a pen. Have everyone list out as many skills as they have or would like to develop on individual sticky notes, stacking a pile in front of them.

Encourage team members to list any and every skill they may have. What tools have they used for previous work projects? Do they have any hobbies? Have they worked on this problem before? Everything is relevant in this ideation phase.

Afterward, talk through all of the sticky notes and place them on a wall or white board, grouping similar skills together.

Based on the skills you've laid out, define some tentative roles for the team. If someone is strong in social media and writing, perhaps they can serve as your expertise engagement lead, finding subject matter experts to connect with for interviews and expert guidance. If another team member is comfortable with data analytics, perhaps they can be in charge of finding relevant data sets and sources that can be used for designing or testing the impact of your proposed solution.

The next week, Sarah, one of her Archways colleagues, and the employees from the other nonprofits met up for their first meeting. The group started out by talking through their backgrounds, professional experiences, skills, and interests.

- *Sarah brought a professional background in nonprofit management; she would keep the team organized and on track. She also had a personal interest in social media marketing and influencing.*
- *Dina, Sarah's colleague from Archways, had worked her way up in the nonprofit. Her first job at Archways was as a client support specialist, working "in the field" with people with mental disabilities day in and day out. She brought an understanding of the unique challenges facing the staff but was also well versed in ways to mitigate behavioral issues. Dina was interested in learning more about the science behind behavioral intervention and volunteered to lead the group's research into the topic.*
- *Tricia was a peer from a nonprofit in the next county, Avenues. She had started out supporting Avenues as an intern, introducing the organization to data management and analysis. She volunteered to serve as the group's data cruncher and statistical researcher.*

- *Salem was a staff trainer from the nonprofit Thoroughfares. His job was to prepare new hires and run them through state- and federally-mandated training programs that were required for the nonprofits to maintain their accreditation. He offered to bring a trainer's perspective and was excited to see how they could "shake things up" and make the training process more impactful for new hires.*
- *Miguel was a behavioral management specialist who worked with Salem at Thoroughfares. Trained in clinical psychology, he was excited about sharing his expertise with the group to help inform new training methods. He had previously served as a researcher at one of the universities in the region, and he offered to help the team connect with academics and researchers on the topic.*

4) BRAINSTORM AS A TEAM

Now it's time to start brainstorming solutions. Remember, this is a time to be creative and outlandish. Don't limit the team—have blue sky conversations about an ideal world where you have all the skills and resources you need and anything is possible. It's okay to get a little crazy!

If you need some ideas of how to brainstorm, refer back to Chapter 9 "Design Thinking—Dreaming to Big Ideas." A few exercises described there can help you get creative.

While you're brainstorming, encourage the team to build upon the ideas of others rather than nix ideas early on; advocate for team members using the "yes and" approach, where they build upon one another's perspectives and ideas. Approach challenges from a perspective of "how might we..." rather than "if only..."

Once again, put all of your ideas down on paper and start to bucket them. Do you have a lot of great ideas around one element of the root problem? Or does your team find itself gravitating toward a particular solution type?

You don't need to decide which solution to pursue during that first brainstorming session. Instead, the team should come away with ideas for further research and exploration. Divvy up topics to team members with related interests and start digging.

After introductions, the team began brainstorming innovative ways to help better prepare staff—or support them—in case of aggressive or erratic behaviors or actions.

"Maybe we could use little robots to distract a client if they begin acting aggressively toward a staff member?"

"What if we gave everybody like a puff up suit thing that they could activate with a button, so if they feel like they're in a dangerous situation, they can puff up and be protected?"

As the group discussed, they found themselves focusing on the experiences of the staff and ways to help them better respond to situations. They agreed to narrow their solution to that topic. As they concluded the initial session, the team agreed to meet with the field staff to get their perspectives

*of what would be helpful to them in challenging or danger-
ous situations.*

5) DO SOME RESEARCH TO NARROW DOWN THE OPTIONS

With roles assigned, work with the team to begin doing some research around your early ideas. Have other groups already tried something similar? If so, why did they succeed or fail? Is there room for improvement on an already existing solution? If it's never been done, can you find any information about why?

Even if you find your solution has been tried before, that shouldn't deter you. If you and your team have a passion for the effort and have the right skill sets, there may be an opportunity for you to do something similar or better. Just because it's been done doesn't mean it's been done (or applied) well! After all, if more of us are trying to help solve a problem, doesn't that increase our likelihood of success?

As you're researching, explore what tools and capabilities you may need to follow through on your idea.

- Do you need a particular type of hardware or building tool?
- Can your team afford to purchase one, or can you find one to borrow for free?
- Do you need a specific skill set or type of expertise to be successful that isn't currently represented on your team?

Research can look like a lot of things. Be willing to explore information you can find in libraries, in scientific journals, or through direct interviews with experts, policymakers, or academics to curate a well-rounded view of the challenge and the solution you're looking to create.

Once you've done your research, come back together as a team to narrow down the options of your initial brainstorm based on what you've learned. Some ideas will get immediately thrown out—they've been done and failed, they're too expensive, they'll require too much specialized equipment.

But others will stand out. Your team will have the skills needed, the passion to explore them, and access to the resources that will be needed to create them.

As you're narrowing down your list, think through the following:

- Likely Impact: Will this idea or solution solve for the root of the problem? What will be the range of the potential impact? Will it help a little bit or a lot?
- Ability to Measure: How can you define success with this idea? Will you be able to measure its success quantifiably, or will it have a less concrete impact? Note that this shouldn't be a disqualifier—many things worth doing aren't yet measurable by hard data—but should be a consideration!
- Tools Needed: Do you have access to everything you'd need to create a prototype or minimum viable product of this idea?

- Time Needed: How long will it take you and your team to create, design, build, and potentially implement this idea? Can the issue at hand wait that long for a solution?
- Resources Needed: How much money will be needed to design, build, and test this? Does your team have access to those types of funds? If not, are there ways you can request funding (state or federal funding, grants, partnerships with professional organizations, etc.)?

Using these criteria as a guide, narrow down your options. Choose one idea to pursue immediately but make a note of three to five other ideas to explore if the first option doesn't pan out. When narrowing in on your solution, remember that **you can go big—for a Moonshot—or you can go small—for a single step—but whatever you choose, go forward.**

When the group reconvened, they had a lot of information to share. "It was incredible," Dina said. "I thought when I talked to the Archways staff about behavioral challenges, they would ask for some tool or something they could use in the moment to diffuse the situation. But time and time again they told me, 'I just wish I were better prepared. I want to help, I just don't know what to do.'"

"We found the same thing at Thoroughfares," shared Miguel. "It really seems like our current methods of training aren't cutting it for people. Nothing can really mimic real-life experience; nothing can replicate being in the moment and

working your own way through it. The team members who were old hats told us, 'I'm great at this job because I've had to learn so much along the way.'"

*"Whatever the case, it's clear our death by PowerPoint trainings isn't enough," sighed Salem. "I mean, what do we do? Create a **new** training just on behaviors? People are already unfocused on the trainings I have to give them now."*

Sarah tapped her finger to the table. "What if there was a way to give people that experience, that in the moment experience, before they even start working?"

"What, like acting or skits or something?" asked Tricia.

"No…I don't think that would really be the same. Maybe shadowing or something?" Sarah replied.

"I don't think that would work either," shared Miguel. "Having two staff could influence behavior or reactions. So we could have someone shadow for weeks and never experience a tense moment, while someone else could be in a tough situation within five minutes."

"What if we could put people into the situations?" Tricia asked. "Simulate them?"

"How do you mean?" asked Dina.

"Are any of you familiar with virtual reality?" Tricia asked.

Tricia proposed using virtual reality headsets—which were becoming increasingly affordable—to drop new hires into challenging environments and give them the opportunity to learn appropriate reactions or responses by doing rather than by sitting through presentations. "We could build a training module that would walk people through what to do in certain situations. We could even build in a test that people have to pass in the simulation to prove they're ready to work with people with mental disabilities."

"That...could really work!"

6) BE WILLING TO LEARN SOMETHING NEW

When you've narrowed down your potential solutions, you may find that you are not familiar with all of the tools that will be needed to begin developing one of the ideas you came to. Even if it's not explicitly aligned to your role on the team, I recommend exploring online courses or other materials to become more comfortable with the concepts and content that will be used to bring your idea to life.

"I'll be honest with you all—I don't know anything about virtual reality, outside of some of the cool videos I've seen online," shared Sarah.

The group agreed to research virtual reality and how it could be used for educational purposes. When they reconvened

7) START WORKING—AND GET TO MINIMUM FUNCTIONALITY

With an idea selected and your team roles identified, it's time to get to work! Work with your team to start building a solution that meets the primary goal of your innovation, even if it lacks all of the bells and whistles your "ideal" solution might include.

As you're building, bring stakeholders and potential users into the fold early on. If you get their ideas and insights during the development and build phase of your efforts, they'll be able to share perspectives that can help shape your final solution, making it more effective in the long run. As you're working, focus on getting feedback every step of the way! Do potential users of the solution find it effective? Is it helpful? Does it actually address the problem or is it a short-term Band-Aid?

Remember, the focus at this point in time should be creating something that addresses the need but isn't fancy or fully fleshed out. In the technology world, this is known as the "minimum viable product." It's not the end state for your idea. Instead, it will let you test your idea against the problem to see if it is making an impact, and it will give you more room to iterate and make improvements moving forward.

Tricia about common behavioral challenges, they outlined five scenarios they would like to simulate in virtual reality.

"So, here's a problem," shared Tricia. "I know how we can get the VR tools themselves—headsets and controllers—but this training we've outlined is really custom. I don't have the background to actually code or build it."

"I think I can help," replied Dina. "I have a friend who has been taking classes at the local community college. I think they have a Game Development certificate. I bet there are people at the college who know what we'd need to do. I'll reach out to them."

The community college professor who managed the Game Development course of study was thrilled to be contacted by a local nonprofit, especially when the group shared their vision for what they wanted to build. He collaborated with instructors to find a few students who had a specific interest in virtual reality game design and had them begin working on the first version of the simulation as a special project for school credit. The working group began including the game designers in their collaboration sessions.

A few weeks later, the first version of the behavioral training simulation was ready to go.

8) SEEK OUT FEEDBACK

Once you have your initial prototype ready to go, it's time to collect feedback from users, stakeholders, and your organization's leaders. I also recommend reaching out to share your progress with any experts or academics you connected with to get their perspective and feedback on what you've built so far.

To gather feedback from direct users, invite some to try what you've built and share real-time feedback with you as they test out the solution. Ask them for recommendations on how to make the solution stronger or ways to tweak it to make it more useful to them.

After you've begun gathering feedback, it's a good idea to update your organization's leadership on the progress you've made. Schedule a meeting with the people who are sponsoring and supporting the initiative and share a status update of how the effort has been going. Let them try the prototype or solution themselves and ask them for their thoughts and feedback on what you've developed so far. While this may not have a long-term impact on the solution itself, keeping the sponsoring leaders up-to-date on what you're working on will help them continue to advocate for the project and share your early successes with other leaders in the field.

step-by-step pop-up boxes recommending actions to take?" suggested one staff member.

They also tested the training with new hires who hadn't yet worked in the field. "This is really cool," shared one new hire, "but a little boring. What if it was like a game? If I got points for picking the **best** option rather than a good option?"

Inspired by the group's previous success collaborating with the community college, Miguel reached out to his former coworkers at a nearby research university and shared the prototype. The university's behavioral psychology professors asked to demo the training to see if the innovation could be more broadly applied to prepare caretakers for behavioral challenges in patients, the elderly, special needs children, and others. They shared recommendations for tweaking the simulations and making them less formulaic.

Meanwhile, Sarah scheduled a meeting for the Archways Director Ben and the other nonprofit leaders. She and the team shared the story of how the initiative was progressing. They invited each attendee to try out the demo training for themselves. Ben was the first to try the simulation. When he took off the virtual reality headset, he paused—then smiled. "That was incredible. It was so vivid, like I was actually in the moment."

"Great job, everyone," said Myra, the Director of Avenues. "This could completely revamp how we train and prepare our staff members. I'm happy to continue providing some funding and staff time to keep exploring this!"

9) ITERATE

After feedback and initial tests, you'll likely note that your MVP isn't performing in quite the way you'd hoped. This is normal and expected!

Take a look at all of the information you've gathered. Collaborate with the team to prioritize it. What pieces of feedback were the most impactful in terms of its *effectiveness at addressing the problem*? With prioritization in hand, begin to identify these critical gaps first and work with the team to figure out how to improve your solution to address them or how to mitigate their impact.

As you're working your way down your list of future iterations, focus your resources and energy on critical needs rather than "nice to haves." If a user has shared feedback that they won't use your solution unless X, explore incorporating X. But if another user says your solution works okay but they'd prefer Y, consider incorporating Y at another time or as resources permit.

While you're refining your solution, encourage the team to get creative with iteration. New feedback and identified shortcomings may require you to go into new rounds of brainstorming of how to incorporate needed features. Don't prioritize the easiest fixes. Remember your initial solution was specifically designed to give you room for future enhancements!

From here, **keep iterating.** You may find your team going into four or five iteration cycles to improve the solution. If you keep your focus on the problem and incorporate relevant feedback from stakeholders, you'll draw closer to a strong solution with each cycle.

Following the early user testing, the group met to talk through the feedback they had received and begin working on the second version of the VR training. "Quite a few people mentioned a pop-up box with reminders or recommendations on the best course of action would have been really valuable," Dina said. "I think it would be great if we could incorporate that."

"That's something we can do for sure," replied Mike, one of the game development students. "If you all could let me know what those pop-up boxes should say, that should be a fairly quick fix."

"Great, let's make that our top priority for the next version," smiled Sarah.

10) KNOW WHEN TO SCRAP

Sometimes all of our ideas and intentions and resources just don't cut it. If you're continuing to iterate and test your solution and you're not having the impact you were hoping for, don't be afraid to put the project on pause and try something else.

Be willing and open to exploring other avenues or building out your other ideas that were placed on the back burner. Even if your initial prototype is never applied to the final solution, that doesn't mean the effort is wasted. You and your team will have learned what *doesn't* work, which is some of the most powerful learning and information that can be found. You will apply those lessons learned to your final solution, and it will be more impactful and meaningful because of them.

11) LAUNCH

By now you've built a prototype or solution, you've gathered user feedback, you've iterated on the initial solution, and all of your testing says what you've built *can* and *does* have an impact on the root problem you've been looking to solve for.

Congratulations! You've *already begun* changing the world. Now it's time to amplify that impact.

When your project is ready for prime time, your path forward will depend on how you got started.

- If your innovation was supported by your workplace in some way, gather up your team and present your progress and your innovation's potential impact to the organization's leadership. When you share what you've accomplished, propose next steps of how to roll out the innovation either through your organization or in partnership with another organization.
- If your innovation was created by a team outside of a workplace setting, consider partnering with other entities (businesses, nonprofits, NGOs, government grants, etc.) to either request further development funding, tweak and roll out the solution, or bring it to the consumer market. In some cases, you may want to even explore using your solution to begin a start-up and explore outside investor funding.

If you have a good idea, and you can prove it will make an impact on the world, you *can and will* find a way to apply it directly to the problem. It may take time and tenacity, but you've already proven that you care enough about this issue to spend both.

If you find yourself stuck, remember—I'm team member number two. You can always reach me at www.techtosavethe-world.com and I'll do my best to help!

A few months later, Archways, Avenues, Thoroughfares, and the two colleges joined forces to launch a new training methodology and simulation: "In the Moment," or ITM Training. The training was rolled out and tested successfully at the three nonprofits, resulting in a significant increase in staff member retention and a reduction of critical incidents.

Following its early success, the training was approved by the state accreditation board for training new staff members at nonprofits throughout the region. With interest in the new training program growing, the group began to charge a small fee for access for the training, which went back to the nonprofits and community college that had initially sponsored the effort.

The community college and the behavioral research center began sharing the tool in their respective technology and research circles, and interest in the module and method grew. Over time, and as virtual reality tools continued to become less expensive, ITM Training began to become common practice at nonprofits serving the mentally disabled—at nursing homes and at hospitals.

13

BLUEPRINT: FOR EXECUTIVES

—

BLUEPRINT FOR EXECUTIVES

Executives are leaders at companies and nonprofits who may not have the time to be in the "day-to-day" of idealistic innovation but who can assign funding, talent, time, and other resources toward a goal. The Executive Blueprint will be useful for nonprofit executives, private sector executives at technology companies with philanthropy goals, government officials, or high-ranking executives in other spaces who want to bring more innovation into their organization. While the characters and stories highlighted in this section are fictitious, they are inspired by real-life idealistic innovation projects.

MEET WILL

1) UNDERSTAND YOUR ROLE IN INNOVATION

As a leader, the role you play in idealistic innovation will be a bit different from an individual contributor. Instead of working on the innovation yourself, your primary role is to create an environment in which innovation can thrive. If you work at a company that has corporate social responsibility goals, or if you work at a nonprofit that can apply technology and innovation directly to further your mission, you have the opportunity to create space for your employees to do incredible things.

Can we find ways to save energy while not negatively impacting our customer experience? If you'd like to explore these questions, send me a note. I'll be setting up a meeting next week."

Will sat back before he sent the email. Just asking people for ideas wouldn't be enough. He'd need to get the right people together in the room to think about ways they could change their business to be more sustainable. After all, while the CEO was only challenging them to reduce their energy use by 5 percent, consumer pressures for sustainable business practices were only growing. In a few years, it may become 10 percent or even 20 percent. What better time than now to dream big?

2) DEMOCRATIZE INNOVATION

As an executive, you're busy and overloaded with information on a daily basis. It can be easy to want to go to people who you know are your top performers for innovation efforts, but by opening up the opportunity to other members of your organization, you may find that you get a more diverse and creative group.

As he prepared to send the note, Will typed in the names of his usual suspects—high performers he knew could deliver solid ideas around the ask. But as he went to click SEND, he paused. Maybe this was an opportunity to get a wide range of ideas from people across all levels.

He reviewed the email and updated some of the verbiage for a broader audience. Then, he updated the TO line to

3) PURSUE LOFTY, TARGETED, GOALS

In Chapter 4 "Collaborating," we discussed the importance of giving people something substantial to collaborate around. You may have driven, talented people in your organization, but they're not going to be inspired to think outside of the box and innovate for something incremental like "increasing profits by 5 percent" or "increasing our market share." Instead, give them something *big* to tackle!

At the same time, many organizations make the mistake of innovating for innovation's sake. Usually, this takes the shape of spending a lot of money on hiring skilled specialists and investing in new technologies that may or may not help the organization actually further its mission. Big data is one of the latest trends in this vein; many companies and non-profits are hiring data scientists, then wringing their hands when the analysts are only able to produce lackluster results because the organization doesn't have well-managed data to draw from.

When bringing idealistic innovation into your organization, try to make the challenges your teams are solving for lofty yet specific. "How might we reduce the amount of water pollution we generate?" or "How might we use technology to measure and track the impact of our coral preservation program?" are examples of lofty, targeted challenges that can be presented to your teams.

Will was surprised to find that his email only received a few responses, but was pleased they seemed to come from people at all levels of the company. He set up a meeting with the five people who shared ideas and a dedicated project manager from his office for the following week.

When the group came together, Will welcomed them and thanked them for their time. The team included a data analyst, a member of the public relations team, a real estate specialist, a pet food nutrition scientist, a supply chain specialist, and the project manager. They were a diverse group with different educational, professional, and personal backgrounds, but they had one thing in common.

"I really love the Global Animal Account, so I wanted to help out with the partnership," shared the real estate specialist.

"I've been hoping the company would take a stance on corporate energy consumption for a long time. I don't know what I really bring because I'm not an expert, but I'm happy to help out," added the nutritional scientist.

"Well, I'm glad you're all passionate about the issue, because we have a big challenge in front of us. I want to figure out how we can reduce our energy use across the organization by 25 percent. I want to turn how we do business upside down and figure out a way to use fewer resources," Will announced.

4) DEDICATE FUNDING AND RESOURCES

The number one way organizational innovation fails is lack of dedicated resources. Many organizations like to tout "all of our employees are innovators" or "we don't dedicate funding to innovation because it's in everything we do."

Unless your employees were specifically hired for research and development, innovation is usually not inherently part of their job. In many cases, organizations point to team members who already have full plates and ask them, "Can you take on a special project?" This isn't necessarily bad practice, but those team members are usually expected to help contribute to the innovation effort *while* continuing to deliver the outcomes required of their day-to-day jobs. Then, even if those teams can propose a truly innovative solution, there's usually no dedicated funding available to bring that solution to scale or actually implement it.

As a leader, the best thing you can do to allow for innovation is set aside funding and employee time for it.

"If you confirm that you are, I'm going to work with your leadership to make sure you have dedicated time to focus on this initiative. I'm also setting aside a small amount of money—five thousand dollars to start—for you to purchase equipment or run any small pilots you may find helpful. You'll also have full access to our organizational data, and I can pull in any technical resources you may need to help explore specific questions around different types of technologies."

The group agreed to support the initiative in the longer term with Will's support and sponsorship. With this agreement, they began the brainstorming process.

5) OFFER SPACE FOR CREATIVITY

In addition to funding and resources, *space* for innovation is key. As previously mentioned, many of your team members are likely heavily focused on their day-to-day jobs rather than future enhancements. Giving them the time and space to think creatively and curiously can pay dividends in terms of helping you meet your corporate social responsibility goals or furthering your missions.

To create space for innovation, consider sponsoring employee time for creativity. This can take the form of employee hackathons, innovation learning hours, or creative thinking time for each employee. You should also work to cultivate an organizational culture that encourages curiosity and failure. Many organizations—businesses and nonprofits alike—are risk averse. This results in team members taking fewer risks, which means they are less likely to learn *and* the organization is less likely to make an innovative breakthrough.

As an executive, you can help set the tone for your organization. Encourage creativity and even productive failure! As Zander Lurie, SurveyMonkey CEO, writes, "If folks aren't failing, they're not asking hard enough questions or taking big enough risks."

As the brainstorming progressed, it became clear to Will that he was inhibiting the discussion. The team brimmed with energy and enthusiasm, but the ideas that were shared were very safe and conventional. He could sense people were holding back out of fear for seeming stupid in front of an executive.

"This has been a great discussion, thank you all. I have to get back for a board meeting, but I would like you all to reconvene tomorrow. I've set aside a large conference room for this group to use as a collaboration space and lab. The project manager will lead a deeper brainstorming discussion and you can begin collaborating from there. I expect some crazy ideas, so please get creative!"

6) REVIEW ORGANIZATIONAL ASPECTS TO CREATE SPACE FOR INNOVATION

Innovation within organizations is limited in a number of ways—by resistance to change, risk aversion, lack of understanding, funding requirements, security requirements, and even by people working in roles that may require more technical acumen than they currently have. If you find your efforts to create space for innovation are less productive than you'd hoped, begin exploring the potential root causes across the organization.

Cybersecurity is a paramount issue for many organizations, but security-related controls and policies can also hinder progress and innovation. As an example, an innovation team may discover that a new application can help a nonprofit capture and share data with other nonprofits doing similar work, but the organization's security policies may require the application undergo an Authority to Operate (ATO) review that can take several months or even years. A secure posture is important, but if it's limiting your ability to use idealistic innovation to further your mission of making the world a better place, it may be time to review your policies.

Regarding risk, many people are risk-averse, and this is especially true in organizations where people hold the same job for long amounts of time. There may be fear of punishment if something fails or goes wrong, or there may even be a sense of "this is how things are done." Work with the teams you oversee to dig into these attitudes to discover where they root and how they can be addressed. As we discussed, failure is one of the greatest learning tools available to us. If you as an executive are open to it, encourage your teams to be as well.

One way to work around risk aversion is the "crawl, walk, run" methodology, where change or innovation is slowly introduced to a team rather than introduced all at once. This methodology allows people to grow accustomed to the idea of a change and share their perspective on how it can be done. This prevents people from feeling as though change has "happened" to them, as they instead shift perspective to feel as though they have contributed to it.

Regarding people, when you're working to build a culture of innovation or ramp up innovation projects, you may find that your teams aren't well-equipped to address the challenge you're facing from a technology perspective. They may have been in their role for a long time, or they just may have never worked with the technology before. Whatever the situation, it's important to remember this is not a shortcoming on your team's part; it's a lack of opportunity.

If you're looking to make a change on your teams, first offer opportunities to your existing team to train up on the skills and technologies that will be used. Offer upskilling opportunities in the form of training or certifications to give them the chance to get up to speed on the technology that will be needed. If they're uninterested in learning, or if it's not something they enjoy, work with them to try to find them a new opportunity somewhere else on the team or in the organization where they can use their expertise to help further the organization's mission.

"Well...it went okay. The group actually came up with a lot of great ideas, but we're not sure how realistic they are," the PM replied.

"Why's that?"

"If I'm being honest, we just aren't sure that some of the more innovative ideas will really work here at PJ. The team had some really incredible and doable ideas, but there are so many barriers...cybersecurity, company culture, the fact that our workforce is scattered all around the country. We're just not sure that something really impactful will succeed."

"I understand," said Will. "But let's take it one step at a time. Let's explore some of those big ideas, and I can work with the team and with company leadership to try and limit the barriers to the ones that seem the most promising."

The project manager smiled. "Okay, I'll let the team know. Thanks for your sponsorship on this. They're really excited."

The next week, the innovation team invited Will to the collaboration space for an update. "Will," said the data analyst, "have you ever heard of smart buildings?"

"I've heard of a smart home. Where your fridge knows that you're out of milk, right?"

The group laughed. "Something like that! A smart building is a combination of technology tools that help people monitor their utility and energy usage, among other things. It uses

Internet of Things sensors to track how energy is being used, how much water is being utilized, and so on. It also allows for what is called remote monitoring or intervention, where you don't have to be at a building to see the status. You could potentially be sitting here at HQ and see the energy consumption of a store in Crawfordsville, Indiana."

"That's pretty cool," replied Will as the team pulled up a visual mock-up of a "PJ Company Energy Consumption Dashboard."

"It gets cooler," replied the supply chain specialist. "Smart buildings can be integrated with building automation systems, so you can not only track how much energy systems are using, but you can also tell the system to use less energy through a variety of settings. So, if you have a fan running all the time in the Crawfordsville location, your smart building will allow you to ask the building system to turn that fan off outside of business hours. Immediate energy savings. Now multiply that by hundreds of locations around the world."

The team walked Will through the components of the solution and even shared a physical demo with him that allowed him to turn off the lights in the office from a mock-up control center on a tablet.

"We think this could be the answer," shared the data analyst. "But we have two big problems. One, we think this will pay for itself over time, but implementing this in all of our locations across the country is going to be a big expense. Two, we're not able to quantify how much energy we will

actually save because we have no way to collect and analyze the baseline data of how much we're burning today outside of utility bills without these sensors in place. We can make a guesstimate, but we won't know for sure."

Will nodded. "I understand. Leave that to me. One question…do we know of anyone else in the retail space who has done something like this?"

7) COLLABORATE FOR GREAT IMPACT

Sometimes, especially in the nonprofit world, our innovative ideas have already been tested by other organizations. When possible, be open to setting aside old rivalries and fears of revealing trade secrets. Reach out to your peers in similar organizations to ask what they've tried and where they've succeeded or failed. Offer to trade gathered data with them and work together to solve challenges when it benefits both parties.

I'm not advocating for you to call up your primary competitor and give them all of your company's proprietary data. In some instances, sharing information and data that don't undermine your own organization's efforts can broaden your collective impact.

"Well, funny you should ask that," said the real estate specialist. "The vendor we were working with on this mentioned they've done similar work for House Haven box stores. They told us there had been major energy savings,

but they couldn't tell us how much without House Haven's permission."

When he returned to his office, Will opened LinkedIn and flipped through his contacts. In a few moments, he found the profile for House Haven's COO, Erin. While they weren't directly connected, they had a few connections in common. Will recognized the names from an industry conference he had attended the year prior. He sent a connection invitation.

Later that week, the two COOs had a quick phone call. "Thanks for making the time," said Will. "PJ is working on an initiative to implement smart buildings technology in our stores to save energy. My team says you've done something similar at House Haven."

"We have!" Erin replied. "Great research by your team. Yes, we got started last year. We're still rolling it out countrywide, but the results have been incredible. We're saving a lot of energy and money."

"I have a favor to ask," said Will. "I have to pitch this to my c-suite, and I know it's going to take a big investment up front. Would you be willing to share some of the data around your results with this initiative? It'd help us get dedicated funding and approval."

*"Well…I don't know. You all aren't direct competitors, but we do have some overlap in some of the products we offer and the markets we target. I think **my** c-suite might have some issues with that."*

"I hear you," said Will. "What would you say if I told you that if we were able to partner on this, House Haven's energy savings could be applauded by the Global Animal Account?"

"I'd say you definitely have my attention," laughed Erin.

8) CHAMPION INNOVATIVE EFFORTS

Your team members can come up with all of the incredible ideas in the world, but they need your help to advocate for their idea, help them get exposure to other parts of the organization, and secure funding for rolling out innovations. You can champion their efforts by carving out time in executive meetings to invite the team to present what they've been working on or implementing organizational changes that will be needed to enable the innovation being proposed. You can also support the team by shielding them from administrative style tasks—including reporting—that burn a lot of time and energy. Allow your innovation tiger team to focus on the creativity and the impact.

Will set up a special presentation about the Innovation Team's smart buildings proposal to the PJ c-suite. During the session, the group presented their idea, highlighted the potential benefits, shared the House Haven example, and proposed a pilot of the initiative at three PJ stores and two distribution centers in different locations.

The CEO was impressed by the initiative but expressed disappointment. "We can't quantify how much energy we'll save if we implement this?" he asked. "I wanted to give some numbers to the Global Animal Account."

"Unfortunately, not yet," replied Will. "But what we can do is share the energy savings achieved by House Haven as our inspiration. We can also implement the sensors and operate normally for a week to create a baseline of data for us to compare to moving forward. We can make that a standard practice if we roll this idea out to other locations to track our true progress."

Later that week, the executive team agreed to fund the pilot initiative. A few months later, collaborating with specialists in the smart buildings field, the pilot launched in the five identified locations. After two weeks of monitoring to collect baseline data, the team began training local champions at each location to use the smart buildings interface and adjust the settings to limit energy consumption in the buildings. Two months later, the energy savings at those locations averaged 37 percent!

The pilot was successful and helped company data analysts project how long it would take for energy expenditure savings to pay for the cost of implementing the new solution. After it was determined that the PJ company would be able to cover up front costs in less than two years, the executive team agreed to roll out the solution to all of their locations across the country.

The announcement of the energy consumption partnership with House Haven and the Global Animal Account was well-received by consumers, and sales increased even *as energy costs decreased. Will rewarded the innovation team with one-time innovation bonuses and continued to invite them back when brainstorming new ideas to address ever-changing corporate priorities.*

Four years later, when the PJ CEO retired, Will was selected to fill the role.

APPRECIATION AND REFERENCES

14

AUTHOR'S NOTE

—

Tech to Save the World started out as a scattered pile of research notes about inspiring technologies that were making the world a better place. I had Post-it Notes all over my desk and on the walls of my office. They were covered in scribbles about idealistic innovation efforts that had caught my eye. Over the course of many months and through countless hours of research and interviews, those scattered thoughts came together to become this conversational guide to changing the world.

I didn't do it alone. It took a community of incredible people to help make this book a reality. I cannot thank them enough for their time and their support but I'm going to try!

To **Matt D. Stevens**, thank you for supporting me through every step of this process. From brainstorming to editing to bringing me coffee as I wrote late into the night, you were a bright spot even on the toughest days. You inspire me to try and make the world a better place every day.

A big thank-you to **Professor Lanier Holt**. As one of my former Journalism professors, Professor Holt's recommendations (and critiques) reshaped the book. Thank you, Professor, for the incredible guidance and the much-needed refresher of your J-200 class!

Will Herbig and Sarah Robb, thank you for being some of my earliest readers and helping me reshape some of the early content! You both kept me focused and helped me home in on what I wanted to say from the time I first sat down to write.

Mary Nichols (Mom), thank you for your support! I know technology isn't your favorite topic, but your thoughts along the way meant a lot to me. Chatting with you about the things I was writing about helped me improve the stories shared in this book.

Professor Jim Bright, thank you for being one of my earliest fans and connecting me with incredible people who were excited to chat with me about idealistic innovation, entrepreneurship, and Design Thinking.

Professor Eric Koester, thank you for inviting me to participate in your Creators Institute. Even though I'd thought about writing a book for years, I wouldn't have had the determination to push through some tough deadlines without your support, guidance, and the broader author community you helped to build.

To **everyone who took the time to meet with me for an interview**, thank you for sharing your story with me and with the readers of this book. I genuinely enjoyed meeting with and learning from each of you. You were pivotal in helping me realize everyone can make a difference in the world and I hope your stories inspire others to action.

To **my team at Accenture,** thank you for your encouragement, support, and curiosity about how we can use *Tech to Save the World.* Chatting with some of you early on helped my ideas around how we can all be world changers and come together.

To all of my **Early Draft readers**, thank you for your detailed feedback (positive *and* constructive)! Your thoughts, questions, and ideas for improvement helped shape the final draft:

Lanier Holt
Matthew D. Stevens
William Herbig
Sarah Robb
Brian J. Bevins
Elijah Ostrow
Levi McAnulty
Irina Karmanova
Mary Nichols
Ben Nichols

To **everyone who preordered _Tech to Save the World,_** thank you for supporting the prelaunch campaign that covered initial printing and distribution costs and made this book a reality:

Matthew D. Stevens
Therese Calhan
Melody Luppino
Jamie Bosse
Levi McAnulty
Marsha E. Lovejoy
Elijah Ostrow
Brian Cluff
Terry Nichols
David Robb
Bill Spiegel
Jim and Janet Zielinski
Richard Torcia
Levi McAnulty
Erica Jaume
Kara Kraus Sundar
Alison Bowers
Deborah C. Howard
Michelle Smith
Leslie Denison
Matt Tamburro
Tyler Skluzacek
Irina Karmanova
Zubin Adrianvala
Sara Burkhart
Benjamin Nichols
Sarah Robb

Cody Leatherman
Edward Bevins
Arthur Coleman
Brian J. Bevins
Eric Koester
Joe Stevens
Mary Nichols
William Herbig
Jennifer Perry
Miguel Zavala
Cathi Bevins
Allison Maranuk
Todd Howard
Robert James Blumer
John Z. Stevens
Hannah Jones
Jason Whitney
Zachary Thomas
Kandora Hargis
Cody Hargis
Chas Gordon
Tiffany Varney
Rima Ziab
Ellie Newberry-Wortham
Brandon Palm
Valorie A. Stevens
David Avasthi
Catharine Minichino
Marina Paul

And finally, **thank you** for reading *Tech to Save the World* and letting me share these stories and dreams for a better future with you. I hope these stories stick with you and inspire you to action the next time you find yourself thinking "someone should do something about that."

15

REFERENCES

———

CHAPTER 1: TECH WON'T SAVE THE WORLD—YOU WILL

- Abrams, Stacey. "3 Questions to Ask Yourself about Everything You Do." Filmed November 2018 in Palm Springs, CA. TED Video. https://www.ted.com/talks/stacey_abrams_3_questions_to_ask_yourself_about_everything_you_do/.

- Centers for Disease Control and Prevention. "Maternal Mortality." Centers for Disease Control and Prevention. Centers for Disease Control and Prevention, August 13, 2020. https://www.cdc.gov/reproductivehealth/maternal-mortality/index.html.

- Gordon, Kim. "Impact Overview - We Care Solar." We Care Solar. October 27, 2020. https://wecaresolar.org/our-impact/impact-overview.

- Hall, Tony P. "Their First Love: The Wright Brothers and Printing." Library of Congress. 2000. http://memory.loc.gov/diglib/legacies/loc.afc.afc-legacies.200002919/.

- Rayome, Alison Denisco. "Why 58% Of Tech Employees Suffer From Imposter Syndrome." TechRepublic. September 7, 2018. https://www.techrepublic.com/article/why-58-of-tech-employees-suffer-from-imposter-syndrome/.

- Root, Rebecca. "Is It Time for Health Facilities to Go Green?" Devex. September 29, 2020. https://www.devex.com/news/is-it-time-for-health-facilities-to-go-green-98098.

- Smithsonian National Air and Space Museum. "Wright Bros., Job Printers." Accessed June 22, 2021. https://airandspace.si.edu/exhibitions/wright-brothers/online/who/1889/printers.cfm.

- Stachel, Laura. "We Care Solar - the Power to Save Lives." We Care Solar. February 15, 2017. https://wecaresolar.org/.

- Stachel, Laura. "Where There Is No Light: A Mixed-Methods Exploration of Quality of Obstetric Care and Energy Access in Low and Middle Income Countries and the Impacts of a 'Solar Suitcase' Intervention," 2020.

- Weir, Leslie. "Press Kit - We Care Solar." We Care Solar. November 19, 2020. https://wecaresolar.org/media/press-kit/.

CHAPTER 2: PUTTING PASSION TO WORK

- "Announcing Fabien Cousteau's PROTEUS ™, a Revolutionary Underwater Scientific Research Station and Habitat Addressing Humanity's Most Critical Concerns." Fabien Cousteau Ocean Learning Center. July 22, 2020. https://www.fabiencousteauolc.org/.

- Bell, Ashley, and John Michael McCarthy III. *Love & Bananas: An Elephant Story*. USA, 2018. http://www.imdb.com/title/tt6069620/.

- Cardon, Melissa S., Joakim Wincent, Jagdip Singh, and Mateja Drnovsek. "The Nature and Experience of Entrepreneurial Passion." *Academy of Management Review* 34, no. 3 (2009): 511–532.

- Jachimowicz, Jon M., Andreas Wihler, Erica R. Bailey, and Adam D. Galinsky. "Why Grit Requires Perseverance and Passion to Positively Predict Performance." *Proceedings of the National Academy of Sciences of the United States of America* 115, no. 40 (2018): 9980–9985.

- Kerpen, Dave. "15 Inspiring Quotes on Passion (Get Back to What You Love)." Inc. March 27, 2014. https://www.inc.com/dave-kerpen/15-quotes-on-passion-to-inspire-a-better-life.html.

- King, Robert. "The Elephant Whisperer." The Ecologist. November 2015.

- "Our Founder." Save Elephant Foundation. Accessed June 22, 2021. https://www.saveelephant.org/about/founder-sangduen-lek-chailert.

- Sinek, Simon. *Start with Why: How Great Leaders Inspire Everyone to Take Action*. Harlow, England: Penguin Books, 2009.

- Teller, Astro. "A Peek inside the Moonshot Factory Operating Manual." X, the Moonshot Factory. July 23, 2016. https://blog.x.company/a-peek-inside-the-moonshot-factory-operating-manual-f5c33c9ab4d7.

- "The Fabien Cousteau Ocean Learning Center." Fabien Cousteau Ocean Learning Center. Accessed January 13, 2021. https://www.fabiencousteauolc.org/.

- "This Was My 'Aha' Moment to Save a Beloved Species." WLFI. April 28, 2018. https://www.wlfi.com/content/national/481094251.html.

- US Department of Commerce, National Oceanic, and Atmospheric Administration. "How Much of the Ocean Have We Explored?" Accessed May 15, 2021. https://oceanservice.noaa.gov/facts/exploration.html.

- Veroniek Collewaert, Frederik Anseel. "How Entrepreneurs Can Keep Their Passion from Fading." *Harvard Business Review*, June 16, 2016. https://hbr.org/2016/06/how-entrepreneurs-can-keep-their-passion-from-fading.

CHAPTER 3: FRAMING THE PROBLEM

- Bregman, Peter. "Are You Trying to Solve the Wrong Problem?" *Harvard Business Review*, December 7, 2015. https://hbr.org/2015/12/are-you-solving-the-wrong-problem.

- Cantero-Gomez, Paloma. "How to Frame a Problem to Find the Right Solution." *Forbes Magazine*, April 10, 2019. https://www.forbes.com/sites/palomacanterogomez/2019/04/10/how-to-frame-a-problem-to-find-the-right-solution/.

- "Human Powered Flight." Royal Aeronautical Society. Accessed May 30, 2021. https://www.aerosociety.com/get-involved/specialist-groups/business-general-aviation/human-powered-flight/.

- Markovitz, Daniel. "How to Avoid Rushing to Solutions When Problem-Solving." *Harvard Business Review*, November 27, 2020. https://hbr.org/2020/11/how-to-avoid-rushing-to-solutions-when-problem-solving.

- Marlin, Daniel. "27 Quotes to Change How You Think about Problems." *Entrepreneur*, April 21, 2017. https://www.entrepreneur.com/article/288957.

- Raskin, Aza. "You Are Solving the Wrong Problem." UX Magazine, May 2011. https://uxmag.com/articles/you-are-solving-the-wrong-problem.

- Vozza, Stephanie. "Three Ways to Reframe a Problem to Find an Innovative Solution." Fast Company. September 8, 2015. https://www.fastcompany.com/3050265/three-ways-to-reframe-a-problem-to-find-innovative-solution.

CHAPTER 4: COLLABORATING

- "21 Collaboration Statistics That Show the Power of Teamwork." Bit.Ai. June 14, 2018. https://blog.bit.ai/collaboration-statistics/.

- "Design Thinking Quotes." InnovationTraining.org. February 1, 2019. https://www.innovationtraining.org/design-thinking-quotes/.

- Gaskell, Adi. "New Study Finds That Collaboration Drives Workplace Performance." *Forbes Magazine*, June 22, 2017. https://www.forbes.com/sites/adigaskell/2017/06/22/new-study-finds-that-collaboration-drives-workplace-performance/.

- Great Big Story. "The Life-Saving Weaving of Bolivia's Indigenous Women." April 25, 2017. Video, 00:15. https://www.youtube.com/watch?v=dHDDQVB2SnE&list=PLMFGVXWuJ1C5JrEgn8FwS8rgDHvcgNsMS.

- Hunt, Vivian, Dennis Layton, and Sara Prince. "Why Diversity Matters." McKinsey & Company. July 24, 2015. https://www.mckinsey.com/business-functions/organization/our-insights/why-diversity-matters.

- Kobayashi, Daisuke, Morris M. Salem, Thomas J. Forbes, Brent M. Gordon, Brian D. Soriano, Vivian Dimas, Bryan H. Goldstein, et al. "Results of the Combined U.S. Multicenter Postapproval Study of the Nit-Occlud PDA Device for Percutaneous Closure of Patent Ductus Arteriosus." *Catheterization and Cardiovascular Interventions: Official Journal of the Society for Cardiac Angiography & Interventions* 93 (4): 645–51.

- Martins, Alejandra. "Los Inventos Del Médico Boliviano Que Salvó Miles de Niños." *BBC Mundo*, October 2, 2014. https://www.bbc.com/mundo/noticias/2014/10/141002_medico_boliviano_corazon_am.

- Ovide, Shira. "The Cult of the Tech Genius." *The New York Times*, August 6, 2020. https://www.nytimes.com/2020/08/06/technology/the-cult-of-the-tech-genius.html.

- Rapaport, Lisa. "Bolivian Women Weave Devices to Patch Holes in Hearts." *Reuters*, March 13, 2018. https://www.reuters.com/article/us-health-heart-device-crafting-idUSKCN1GP309.

- Reyes, Ignacio de los. "The Bolivian Women Who Knit Parts for Hearts." *BBC*, March 29, 2015. https://www.bbc.com/news/health-32076070.

- Thelwell, Kim. "Franz Freudenthal." Borgen Project. Accessed June 20, 2021. https://borgenproject.org/tag/franz-freudenthal/.

- Thomas-Aguilar, Blakely. "New Infographic: Studies Reveal Real Benefits of Teamwork & Business Collaboration." PGI. March 26, 2015. https://www.pgi.com/blog/2015/03/infographic-benefits-of-teamwork-collaboration/.

CHAPTER 5: LISTENING AND LEARNING

- Brocklehurst, Clarissa, and Peter Harvey. "An Evaluation of the PlayPump® Water System as an Appropriate Technology for Water, Sanitation and Hygiene Programmes." https://www-tc.pbs.org/frontlineworld/stories/southernafrica904/flash/pdf/unicef_pp_report.pdf.

- Overland, Martha Ann. "He Designed a Smartwatch App to Help Stop His Dad's Nightmares." *NPR*, December 6, 2020.

https://www.npr.org/2020/12/06/943647610/he-designed-a-smartwatch-app-to-help-stop-his-dads-nightmares.

- Stellar, Daniel. "The PlayPump: What Went Wrong?" Columbia University. July 1, 2010. https://news.climate.columbia.edu/2010/07/01/the-playpump-what-went-wrong/.

- Thomsen, Dave. "Why Human-Centered Design Matters." *Wired*, December 20, 2013. https://www.wired.com/insights/2013/12/human-centered-design-matters/.

- "Troubled Water." *Frontline/World*. PBS. https://www.pbs.org/video/frontlineworld-troubled-water/.

- "Troubled Water." FRONTLINE/World. June 29, 2010. https://www.pbs.org/frontlineworld/stories/southernafrica904/video_index.html.

CHAPTER 6: ITERATING

- Anthony, Scott D. "Innovation and Iteration: Friends Not Foes." *Harvard Business Review*, May 12, 2008. https://hbr.org/2008/05/innovation-and-iteration-frien.

- Ashkenas, Ron. "When Failure Is a Good Option." *Harvard Business Review*, August 14, 2012. https://hbr.org/2012/08/when-failure-is-a-good-option.

- Cohen, Taya. *Why Do We Hate to Fail?* WHYY. PBS & NPR. https://whyy.org/segments/why-do-we-hate-to-fail/.

- Obama, Michelle. *Becoming.* New York: Crown Publishing Group, 2018.

- Palermo, Elizabeth. "Who Invented the Light Bulb?" Live Science. August 17, 2017. https://www.livescience.com/43424-who-invented-the-light-bulb.html.

- Taylor, Bill. "How Coca-Cola, Netflix, and Amazon Learn from Failure." *Harvard Business Review,* November 10, 2017. https://hbr.org/2017/11/how-coca-cola-netflix-and-amazon-learn-from-failure.

CHAPTER 7: LET'S GET TO WORK

- Kendall, Graham. "Apollo 11 Anniversary: Could an iPhone Fly Me to the Moon?" *Independent,* July 15, 2019. https://www.independent.co.uk/news/science/apollo-11-moon-landing-mobile-phones-smartphone-iphone-a8988351.html.

- Poniewozik, James. "Parks and Recreation Watch: Find Your Team and Get to Work." *Time,* February 24, 2015. https://time.com/3720581/parks-and-recreation-finale-review-recap/.

CHAPTER 8: BUILDING COMFORT WITH TECHNOLOGY

- Briggs, Saga. "25 Ways to Develop a Growth Mindset." InformED. February 10, 2015. https://www.opencolleges.edu.au/informed/features/develop-a-growth-mindset/.

- LaFrance, Adrienne. "When People Feared Computers." *Atlantic Monthly*, March 30, 2015. https://www.theatlantic.com/technology/archive/2015/03/when-people-feared-computers/388919/.

- Limeri, Lisa B., Nathan T. Carter, Jun Choe, Hannah G. Harper, Hannah R. Martin, Annaleigh Benton, and Erin L. Dolan. "Growing a Growth Mindset: Characterizing How and Why Undergraduate Students' Mindsets Change." *International Journal of STEM Education* 7, no. 1 (2020). https://doi.org/10.1186/s40594-020-00227-2.

- Romm, Cari. "Americans Are More Afraid of Robots than Death." *Atlantic Monthly*, October 16, 2015. https://www.theatlantic.com/technology/archive/2015/10/americans-are-more-afraid-of-robots-than-death/410929/.

CHAPTER 9: DESIGN THINKING—DREAMING TO BIG IDEAS

- Brown, Tim. "Design Thinking." *Harvard Business Review*, June 1, 2008. https://hbr.org/2008/06/design-thinking.

- Carrington, Damian. "Orca 'Apocalypse': Half of Killer Whales Doomed to Die from Pollution." *The Guardian*, September 27, 2018. http://www.theguardian.com/environment/2018/sep/27/orca-apocalypse-half-of-killer-whales-doomed-to-die-from-pollution.

- Deichmann, Dirk, and Roel van der Heijde. "How Design Thinking Turned One Hospital into a Bright and Comforting

- Place." *Harvard Business Review*, December 2, 2016. https://hbr.org/2016/12/how-design-thinking-turned-one-hospital-into-a-bright-and-comforting-place.

- "Design Thinking Quotes." Innovation Training. February 1, 2019. https://www.innovationtraining.org/design-thinking-quotes/.

- Hart, Hugh. "Yes, and … 5 More Lessons in Improving Collaboration and Creativity from Second City." Fast Company. February 26, 2015. https://www.fastcompany.com/3042080/yes-and-5-more-lessons-in-improv-ing-collaboration-and-creativity-from-second-city.

- "How Might We." Design Kit. Accessed April 22, 2021. https://www.designkit.org/methods/3.

- "Killer Whale." NOAA Fisheries. Accessed April 5, 2021. https://www.fisheries.noaa.gov/species/killer-whale.

- Janosch, Brian. "No Joke! Yes, You Can Learn from How the Onion Brainstorms Its Ideas." TEDx Talk. March 18, 2019. https://ideas.ted.com/how-did-the-chicken-reach-the-great-idea-she-borrowed-the-onions-techniques-for-brainstorming/.

- Liedtka, Jeanne. "Why Design Thinking Works." *Harvard Business Review*, September 1, 2018. https://hbr.org/2018/09/why-design-thinking-works.

- Muller-Roterberg, Christian. "Design Thinking: Analyzing the Task - Dummies." Dummies. May 31, 2020. https://www.dummies.com/careers/business-skills/design-thinking-analyzing-the-task/.

- Peters, Joost. "Why You Should Get Started with Design Thinking Too." RSM. September 2020. https://www.rsm.nl/executive-education/article/why-you-should-get-started-with-design-thinking-too/.

- Smithsonian. "Fishing with Dynamite." Accessed March 6, 2021. https://ocean.si.edu/ecosystems/coral-reefs/fishing-dynamite.

CHAPTER 10: (SOME OF) THE TOOLS OF INNOVATION

- Bushwick, Sophie. "What the Capitol Riot Data Download Shows about Social Media Vulnerabilities." *Scientific American*, January 27, 2021. https://www.scientificamerican.com/article/what-the-capitol-riot-data-download-shows-about-social-media-vulnerabilities/.

- Chan, Rosalie. "The 10 Most Popular Programming Languages, according to the Microsoft-Owned GitHub." *Business Insider*, November 9, 2019. https://www.businessinsider.com/most-popular-programming-languages-github-2019-11.

- Eastwood, Brian. "The 10 Most Popular Programming Languages to Learn in 2021." Northeastern.Edu. June 18, 2020. https://www.northeastern.edu/graduate/blog/most-popular-programming-languages/.

- Firozi, Paulina. "Thousands of Eggs Abandoned after a Drone Scares off Nesting Birds." *Washington Post*, June 7, 2021. https://www.washingtonpost.com/science/2021/06/07/drone-crash-abandoned-eggs/.

- Goodwill Community Foundation. "The Now: What Is a Drone?" GCF Global. Accessed December 15, 2020. https://edu.gcfglobal.org/en/thenow/what-is-a-drone/1/.

- Hilbert, Martin, and Priscila López. "The World's Technological Capacity to Store, Communicate, and Compute Information." *Science (New York, N.Y.)* 332, no. 6025 (2011): 60–65.

- Hill, Kashmir. "How Target Figured Out a Teen Girl Was Pregnant before Her Father Did." *Forbes Magazine*, February 16, 2012. https://www.forbes.com/sites/kashmirhill/2012/02/16/how-target-figured-out-a-teen-girl-was-pregnant-before-her-father-did/.

- Looper, Christian de, and Andrew Martonik. "What Is 5G? The Next-Gen Mobile Network Is Here." Digital Trends. June 7, 2021. https://www.digitaltrends.com/mobile/what-is-5g/.

- McCarthy, John. "What Is AI? / Basic Questions." Stanford University. 2012. http://jmc.stanford.edu/artificial-intelligence/what-is-ai/index.html.

- *Merriam-Webster.com Dictionary*, s.v. "data," accessed February 2, 2021, https://www.merriam-webster.com/dictionary/data.

- "Mobile Technology." IBM. April 27, 2020. https://www.ibm.com/topics/mobile-technology.

- Rosenberg, Stacy. "Smartphone Ownership Is Growing Rapidly around the World, But Not Always Equally." Pew Research. February 5, 2019. https://www.pewresearch.org/global/2019/02/05/smartphone-ownership-is-growing-rapidly-around-the-world-but-not-always-equally/.

- SAS Institute Inc. "Artificial Intelligence." SAS. June 18, 2021. https://www.sas.com/en_us/insights/analytics/what-is-artificial-intelligence.html.

- Shacklett, Mary. "Artificial Intelligence Can't Yet Learn Common Sense." TechRepublic. May 13, 2020. https://www.techrepublic.com/article/artificial-intelligence-cant-yet-learn-common-sense/.

- Somers, James. "The Pastry A.I. That Learned to Fight Cancer." *New Yorker,* March 18, 2021. https://www.newyorker.com/tech/annals-of-technology/the-pastry-ai-that-learned-to-fight-cancer.

- The Atlantic. "One Solution to Rhino Poaching: Use Sensors to Monitor the Other Animals." *Atlantic Monthly.* Accessed June 24, 2021. https://www.theatlantic.com/sponsored/ibm-2018/rhino-poaching/1880/.

- U.S. Bureau of Labor Statistics. "Web Developers and Digital Designers." U.S. Bureau of Labor Statistics. April 9, 2021. https://www.bls.gov/ooh/computer-and-information-technology/web-developers.htm.

- Villasenor, John. 2012. "What Is a Drone, Anyway?" Scientific American. December 4, 2012. https://blogs.scientificamerican.com/guest-blog/what-is-a-drone-anyway/.

- Visalli, Morgan, Briana Abrahms, and Ana Širović. "This New Technology Can Save Whales from Ship Collisions." World Economic Forum. Accessed June 24, 2021. https://www.

weforum.org/agenda/2020/09/this-new-technology-can-save-whales-from-ship-collisions/.

- Wang, Yue. "More People Have Cell Phones Than Toilets, U.N. Study Shows." *Time*, March 25, 2013. https://newsfeed.time.com/2013/03/25/more-people-have-cell-phones-than-toilets-u-n-study-shows/.

- "Why Amazon, UPS and Even Domino's Is Investing in Drone Delivery Services." *Business Insider*, February 12, 2020. https://www.businessinsider.com/drone-delivery-services.

CHAPTER 11: BLUEPRINT: FOR DREAMERS

- Clark, Dorie. "6 Ways to Convince Someone to Collaborate with You." *Harvard Business Review*, December 15, 2020. https://hbr.org/2020/12/6-ways-to-convince-someone-to-collaborate-with-you.

CHAPTER 12: BLUEPRINT: FOR PROFESSIONALS

- Clark, Dorie. "6 Ways to Convince Someone to Collaborate with You." *Harvard Business Review*, December 15, 2020. https://hbr.org/2020/12/6-ways-to-convince-someone-to-collaborate-with-you.

- Di Fiore, Allesandro, and Elisa Farri. "Seven Tasks for Innovation-Focused Executives." *The Globe and Mail*, August 17, 2016. https://www.theglobeandmail.com/report-on-business/careers/leadership-lab/seven-tasks-for-innovation-focused-executives/article31147183/.

- "Gartner Reveals the Top Three Barriers to Innovation in Marketing." Gartner. November 11, 2019. https://www.gartner.com/en/newsroom/press-releases/2019-11-11-gartner-reveals-the-top-three-barriers-to-innovation-.

- Lurie, Zander. "SurveyMonkey's CEO on Creating a Culture of Curiosity." *Harvard Business Review*, January 1, 2019. https://hbr.org/2019/01/surveymonkeys-ceo-on-creating-a-culture-of-curiosity.